The Angel Inn, Broadway, Worce.

The story of the evolution of a 17th Century building, 1660 to 2022, looking back at the stage and mail coaching era, and Broadway's many inns, beer, ale and cider houses.

Elizabeth Eyre, BA Hons, B.E.M.

This book began as a way of recognising the generosity of the late John Keil of H. W. Keil Ltd, the respected antique dealer and owner of the Tudor House, previously The Angel Inn, now Broadway Museum and Art Gallery. In 2008 John became a co-founder of Broadway's Museum and Art Gallery. I am grateful to him for some of the information on the building's more recent history and all the trustees and volunteers who have supported the Museum since its actual opening in September 2013.

1st Edition 2022

This edition is only a starting point; others are invited to add to Broadway's and the Angel's story.

Disclaimer

This book covers my research, over several years, into the history of Tudor House, 65 High Street, Broadway. It was built as an inn to serve the route from London to Ireland via Worcester and Aberystwyth; the latter was spelt both the Welsh and English way over the years in various historical documents.

I have, wherever possible, triangulated evidence and used source documents. As a result, I believe the contents to be, as far as possible for this first book, accurate. I appreciate that this book is a starting point and that further evidence may shed more light on specific events or facts.

The past is always a puzzle; it would be pleasing to think a second edition might incorporate additional information from deeds in private hands.

Acknowledgements

The late John Keil contacted me in 2008 to ask for my support and assistance in converting one of his buildings in Broadway, Tudor House, into a museum. In addition to his desire for the Museum to house his father's 17th Century Museum pieces, he expressed a wish that the venture might contribute to Broadway's tourism offer, given the tricky economic downturn at that time.

My husband, Douglas, accepted that the long hours of research and writing would preoccupy me. When required, he supported me further, producing sketches, layouts, and illustrations to illuminate and clarify the text.

Jerold Northrop Moore, an American-born, long term Broadway resident, best known for his biography and other writings on the life and music of Sir Edward Elgar, a family friend who has shared his experience as a writer and given me gentle encouragement over the years.

Hans Thormann, an American world traveller and friend, who arrived at our home in Cheltenham in 2021 just when I needed an independent proof-reader.

To Jayne Bridges, a good friend and professional editor who has helped me polish the final document.

To Nigel Smith and his colleagues at Vale Press, who have helped and guided me in producing and printing this book.

First Published in 2022 by
Vale Press,
6 Willersey Business Park,
Willersey WR12 7RR

www.valegroup.co.uk

All rights reserved.

No part of this publication may be reproduced or transmitted in any form or by any means electronic or mechanical including photocopy, recording, or any information storage and retrieval system without permission in writing from the author.

A catalogue record for this book is available from the British Library.
ISBN 978-1-7398400-0-6

Historical research and text written copyright retained by the author
©Elizabeth Eyre 2022

All illustrations and artwork drawn and provided by Doug Eyre; copyright retained by the artist ©Doug Eyre 2022

Contents

Preface 6

4

The Angel Inn, Broadway
(Tudor House, 65 High Street, Broadway)

Preface

In Broadway, the past is ever-present to residents and visitors alike. It is just there. For twenty years, I have researched the history of Broadway and been more than intrigued; I have wanted to awaken the dead, to tease out more. This book is my first tentative step in doing just that. Over time, more details will come to light. I hope this book and those that follow, covering the history of Broadway in Worcestershire, its buildings, its people, and its social and economic drivers for change, will encourage others to do the same. However, there is never just one version of events; history seems to be an inherently messy business.

Writing about the history of a person, family, building, or place requires access to a wealth of legal and social documents and, if possible, eyewitness accounts. Wills, inventories, newspaper articles, references in archives, books no longer in print and manuscripts have enabled me to piece together this first edition. It covers the history of the old house, formerly known as the Angel Inn, now Tudor House, on Broadway's long, broad, High Street. To add context, some of the critical moments in Broadway's 190-year stage, then mail coaching history is included. Information on Broadway's inns, ale, beer, and cider houses is included as an appendix, but it is still a work in progress.

The book covers the main events and players associated with the history of the Angel. In addition, it introduces glimpses of innkeeping in the 17th and the times from its build in 1659 - 1660, in the 17th Century, to today.

Situated as it is in Middle England, Broadway's evolution follows England's history. Tracing one building's ownership and uses seemed to be a good starting point for understanding the settlement's development over the same period. Who owned, leased and managed property throughout history is always a challenge for any historian due to the various land and property recording and conveyancing methods over the years?

Following the Norman Conquest, in 1066, all the land of England was technically owned by the Crown; by 1086, of the fourteen hundred Lords in Chief, only two were English. Under the feudal manorial system, the Crown made grants of land to these foreign earls, barons, and dukes who granted smaller areas to knights in return for active military service in the field: 'knight-service'.

The Lord, the Abbot of Pershore, was the dominant landowner, tenant in chief, in Broadway by the early medieval period. Most villagers living in Broadway would have been freemen[1] however there remained several serfs; land usage was through rights as tenants or under-tenants. Significant under-tenants could have had deeds and documents. Still, for the majority, the method of transferring land from one tenant to another at this time was by 'livery of seisin', a symbolic act whereby a piece of the property, usually a turf or clod of earth, was transferred from one to another witnessed by the community. Such a simple ceremony was a workable system because most people in a settlement knew each other, and the population was generally static. The exchange was then entered in the manorial roll. The copyholder[2] would deliver a rod or wand to the Lord of the Manor or his steward, who would pass it to the new tenant. Recording the event was not always necessary – this is a challenge when tracing Broadway's history.

In addition, before 1660, as now, people looked for ways to avoid the taxes payable to the feudal lord. Following such public acts, they looked for ways in which land might be conveyed secretly to avoid fees. This aspect is an additional challenge when tracing ownership.

After 1066, particularly during the mid 12th Century, many men, barons and freemen, and numerous towns were stripped of their wealth and enslaved[3] to do the bidding of the incumbent invaders.[4]

Later in the Middle Ages, it became commonplace to provide evidence of transactions through a deed of feoffment (possession) or, in the case of copyhold, by an entry on the court rolls. Sometimes such documents still survive.

---

1. A class of peasant, tenant-worker who was not bound to the land, but instead paid rent in exchange for residence. Freemen were free to take their services to other manors or villages if they pleased.
2. So named as the " title deed " received by the tenant was a copy of the relevant entry in the manorial court roll.
3. The reign of King Stephen between 1139 and 1153 is often referred to as The Anarchy.
4. *The Anglo Saxon Chronicles*.

Feudal tenure was finally abolished in 1660, after the Civil War, at the time the Angel was built. With the historic ecclesiastical traditions finally giving way to new scientific, technical, and economic drivers and an increase in the movement of people around the Country, improved methods of recording 'formal title' to property were necessary. Deeds, wills, and inventories were used to clarify ownership, tenancies, or sub tenancies. Transfers were not always the transfer of title to land and property; they might have been a transfer of a lease.

When researching this period, additional challenges were the lack of formal spelling rules before the 18th Century and the extravagant writing style, secretary hand, used in most more legal documents. The absence of punctuation also made source documents hard to read.

Despite the obstacles, Tudor House, 65 High Street, one of Broadway's most stunning Grade 2* heritage buildings, now home to Broadway Museum and Art Gallery, deserved to have its history told. Additionally, it seemed necessary, as far as possible, that elements of Broadway's 190 years as a significant coaching stage, then mail stop, were further documented.

When writing this book, at all stages triangulating the evidence, I bore in mind the Russian adage 'nobody lies like an eyewitness'…. Ask three people to recount one event, and each story will be different.

Elizabeth Eyre 2022

Chapter 1
England at the time of the Inn's construction
Pre 1659-1660

The Protectorate: Oliver Cromwell

Autumn 1642 to autumn 1651 saw the English Civil War play out a series of armed conflicts and political machinations in numerous locations, between the English Parliament, the Parliamentarians ('Roundheads') led by Oliver Cromwell and Charles I, cousin of Queen Elizabeth I, and his supporters, (Royalists).

Cromwell's government was established after a win for the Parliamentarians at nearby Worcester, which led to the execution of Charles I by beheading, 30 January 1649.

The Protectorate period lasted nearly ten years until Cromwell's death, 3 September 1658. His eldest son Richard, nicknamed Tumbledown Dick, took on the mantle but was no match for his father; his unsuccessful reign ended only nine months into office, on

25 May 1659, leaving Parliament to pick up the pieces and resume power.

Within a year, Parliament was reaching out to Charles I's son, Charles II, who arrived back in London on 29 May 1660; the Stuart monarchy had returned to the kingdoms of England, Scotland, and Ireland.

This period, from Charles I's execution to Charles II return, known as the Interregnum, was followed by the Restoration from 1660 to 1685. The Angel's story starts at the time of the Restoration, the year before Charles II returned, a time of considerable change. Charles II fervently embraced the scientific age, an age that created some of the intellectual tensions of the 17th Century.

The country welcomed the overthrow of Puritan 'grimness and dreary disapproval of pleasure'. The promise of stability, facilitated by the newly established political settlement, was a key contributor to a sudden, substantial expansion of travel around the County. Even before Charles II returned from the continent, the writing was on the wall, and plans were being made for coaching routes, organised in stages, between major towns and cities; plans which necessitated accommodation and hospitality along the way.

The Angel was purpose-built between 1659-1660, for the stage midway between Pershore and Moreton in the Marsh, on the route from London to Aberystwyth (spelt the English way, Aberistwith, on several documents). It is now acknowledged that in the 17th Century, given a high tide, ships and boats could sail to and from Ireland from the town[5].

The reassuring name, the Angel, was frequently adopted by inns early on in coaching as this mode of travel was seen as very risky.

---

5. The sand bar in 1660 would appear to have been a barrier, but the castle and the harbour were built in the 13th Century with stone shipped in from Tenby.

Chapter 2
Travel before the expansion of Coaching
11th – 17th Century

Post boys carried mail around the Country – mature experienced men, often ex-military
©Doug Eyre

From the 11th Century, if not before, the primary way of conveying letters: news of battles, and royal edicts, had been via a messenger, a 'post boy' on foot or horseback. To improve communications, Henry VIII, circa 1512, appointed his secretary, Sir Brian Tuke, (c 1490-1545) to 'Master of the Posts'.[6]

Sir Brian Tuke- attributed to Hans Holbein c 1527 - Courtesy National Gallery of Art, Washington

---

6. A date said by some to be the foundation of the postal service in England.

Sir Brian began his role by organising relays of horses and messengers on essential routes. Officially, only the Court could use this service, but increasingly private letters were carried as the Tudor era progressed. After his appointment, the long-awaited improvement plan disappointingly only centred around improving stabling arrangements and the availability of horses.

Throughout the Middle Ages, most people walked, primarily short local distances; roads were poor, little more than tracks. Sadly, the magnificent engineered Roman networks and the 'Saltstrets' had failed to be maintained adequately when the Romans left Britain. If a long journey was necessary, the able-bodied, with sufficient funds, either hired or used their horses and rode. If goods needed to be transported from place to place, wheeled vehicles, usually two-wheeled, were used: wheelbarrows, simple hand carts, horse or bullock drawn carts.

A horse-drawn cart with load, 14th Century

In towns, the infirm or those of a delicate disposition might be carried in a litter or litter bed (a carriage, sometimes curtained, hung on poles, carried by men) or by horse litter (with two horses). This mode of travel, ideal for short distances, could be found in some places from the 15th Century right up to the 19th Century.

Water was a more comfortable means of travel for people of means[7] and merchants, who needed to move heavier goods; It was a popular option, particularly in the summer months when flooding was less likely.

References to coaches can be found from the 13th Century. The first crude depiction of a coach, not a stage coach, was in a manuscript of that century. A century later, 25 September 1355, Elizabeth de Burgh, Lady Clare, bequeathed her *"great carriage, with the covertures, carpets, and cushions"* to her eldest daughter. Carriage-builders at the close of Edward III.'s reign (1327 to 1377) charged between £100 - £1,000 for their wares.[8]

Beyond the coaches built for royal or titled clients, rudimentary coaches started to be built from the 16th Century onwards. However, they were little better than covered wagons, generally drawn by four horses, a combination of leather straps, and crude chairs, with no suspension. Moreover, a journey would be a tedious, miserable affair given that coaches travelled on unmade roads or rutted tracks at less than 5 miles an hour.

An Elizabethan coach with leather strap suspension, no brakes – Tring Local History Museum

---

7. Poet William Campden writing about the funeral of Elizabeth I said, "The Queen was brought by water to Whitehall, at every stroke of oars did tears fall".
8. Charles G. Harper: *Stage coach and mail in days of yore: a picturesque history of the coaching age,* Volume 1, London, Chapman & Hall, Limited, 1903.
.

If funds were no object, it could be a different matter; the sumptuousness of Queen Mary's journey from the Tower of London to Westminster on her Coronation Day, 20 September 1553, in her state coach, is well recorded.

Comfort depended upon suspension. Leaf spring suspension, though crude, was known to the Egyptians and Romans; they later used them on their chariots to absorb shock when riding on rough surfaces. In Hungary, a breakthrough came in the 15th Century when a wheelwright in a village called Kocs, known for building carts and transporting goods between Vienna and Budapest, devised a larger, more comfortable carriage incorporating leaf steel spring suspension. This carriage became known as a *Koczi szeter*, meaning a 'wagon of Kocs, a word later shortened to '*kocsi*,' or coaches.[9] [10]

Carriages were rarely used in England until 1555.[11] Then, in 1564, William Boonen, a Dutchman, brought from the Netherlands a coach, which was presented to Queen Elizabeth.[12] Reports of innovative Dutch Springs and the first horse-drawn coach introduced to England from Holland seem to link back to this date. Indeed, improved spring design led to increased coach building, coaching, and allied trades from around this period.

From the start, prejudices against coaching had to be overcome. The monied and trading class initially thought coaching suspect: vulgar, a way to spread disease, a 'confusion' of rank and class. With whom might one be mixing? Slowly anxieties were surmounted; the sheer

---

9. Oxford English Dictionary.
10. The meaning of coach, as an instructor or trainer, is purportedly from around 1830, when it was Oxford University slang for a tutor who 'carried' a student through an exam; the term 'coaching' was later applied in the 1800's to improving the performance of athletes.
11. John Stow: *A Summarie of the Chronicles of England Diligently Collected, Abridged, & Continued Unto this Present Yere of Christ* 1598.
12. John Taylor, who dubbed himself the "Water Poet," in his life of Thomas Parr, states that Parr was 81 years old "before there was any coach in England." Parr was born in 1483.

convenience of this new way of travelling in town, particularly for the ladies, was a helpful catalyst.

A fare structure was devised to overcome the mixing of the classes and the spreading of diseases; those who could afford the best seats travelled inside the coach, everyone else had to travel on the coach, but outside. For those fortunate enough to travel inside, the fare could be as much as £4.00 plus a few shillings for tips; this was at a time when a labourer might be earning eleven shillings a week. Those paying a reduced fare, which was still expensive, travelled in the rear basket or on the coach roof. They took their life in their hands and clung to ropes or any available grab handle.

The early curved roof designs on coaches would, later, be replaced by a flatter style; the basket was abandoned as luggage flew out and non-paying passengers were known to jump in, as the coach set off. In addition, the rails would be added to enable more passengers on the roof.

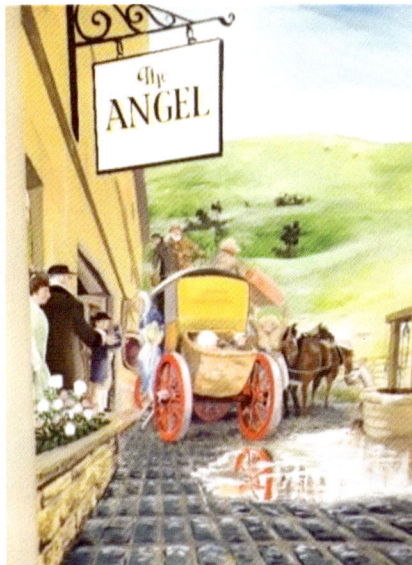

A mid 17th Century stage coach design with its domed roof and basket on the rear; a design which would change to accommodate more passengers over time ©Doug Eyre

Coach design, in 1800: flat roof, grab handles, and box seats to accommodate more passengers Courtesy Royal Mail

Despite a brief resurgence of the plague from 1580 - 1595, particularly in London 1592 - 1593, nothing could stop the steady proliferation of the horse-drawn coaches in towns. Carriages were available for hire in the streets of London from 1605, and the first hint of traffic jams was recorded.[13]

The first fare-paying stage coach route ran from Edinburgh to Leith. Around 1610, a gentleman from the wilds of Pomerania, on the Baltic Sea, obtained a Royal patent granting him the exclusive right of running coaches or waggons, between Edinburgh and Leith, for a term of fifteen years!

There were still those who were not fans. For example, a travel writer in 1617 wrote: *"Covered waggons in which passengers are carried to and fro. This kind of journeying is very tedious so that only women and people of inferior condition travel in this sort...."* [14]

---

13. Gascoigne, Bamber. *HistoryWorld. History of Transport and Travel.*
14. Shakespeare's Europe: *Unpublished chapters of Fynes Moryson's Itinerary (at the time of James I). Being a survey of the condition of Europe at the end of the 16th Century,* transcribed by Charles Hughes, 1903.

Eventually, in 1635, Charles I introduced the 'Letter Office of England and Scotland' plus an official public mail service to increase his revenues. The public was now encouraged to pay his messengers to carry letters, from one 'post' to the next 'post' by carriers on foot or horseback. To develop the network, Charles appointed a merchant, and MP, Thomas Withering's who had previously distinguished himself as the King's 'Postmaster General for Foreign Parts' to Postmaster of England and Scotland.[15]

As for coaching, despite growing numbers and routes, there seemed to have been few technical improvements after the first quarter of the 17th Century, until about 1640, seventy-six years after the first sprung coach of 1564. Then, just as new ideas were coming forward, the whole concept of coaching had to be put on the back burner due to the Civil War, 1642 to 1651. During the war, travel by coach was no longer safe. Cromwell caused a significant stir by taking a coach into Bristol in 1649.

Post the Civil War, the Reformation enabled effort and investment to focus on coaching: improving the infrastructure for stage coaches and their passengers, creating new routes, ensuring improved accommodation, and hopefully roads. Any concerns of gentlemen and traders about coaching melted away due to sheer business necessity. Trade and new opportunities were beckoning.

Simultaneously, in 1657, the "Letters Office" renamed the "Post Office of England" by Act of Parliament, was re-established, and the office of Postmaster-General was defined as "*the exclusive right of carrying letters and the furnishing of post-horses*". None but duly authorised persons were permitted to supply horses. The charge for an able horse was 2½d a mile, rising to 3d by 1658. However, the legislative and practical changes were so rapid that the 1658

---

15. J Wilson Hyde: *The Post in Grant and Farm*, Adam and Charles Black, London 1894.

monopoly, restricting who could supply horses for the carrying of letters, was soon abolished.

When plans for a stage in Broadway and the building of the Angel were drawn up, businesses in the village would have found themselves galvanised to take advantage of this new trade. New equipment would have been acquired to service the associated trades: farriers, blacksmiths, those providing stabling, and the extra horses needed for the long pull up Broadway Hill,[16] maltsters, brewhouse owners and accommodation providers.

Not all traders and villagers would have been equally pleased; there would likely have been a faction resistant to change; it is known that innkeepers who supplied horses for the letter riders despised the new-fangled coaches.[17]

The one aspect of infrastructure which held the industry back was the appallingly poor structure of all roads. Whilst horse riders could easily cut access across any land, thus saving time, coaches could not, and accessible routes were few and far between. Additionally, during cold or wet weather, coach travel was at times impossible or even more hazardous, overloading was a regular risk, and accidents were frequent. To add danger to danger, seeing an opportunity, robbers took advantage of their slow speeds, particularly when passengers had to walk alongside the coach as they went up a hill.

It is hardly surprising that before embarking on a journey, passengers were encouraged to put their affairs in order, make a will and pray hard.

16. The hill nearest to the A44 has been referred to as Fish Hill since the summer house on Broadway Hill was converted to an Inn called the Fish.
17. Charles G. Harper: *The Holyhead Road Vol 1, The Mail-Coach Road to Dublin*, Chapman, and Hall, 1902.

Chapter 3
The start of Stage Coaching in Broadway -
The 'Aberistwith' to London Route
1660

Post the Civil War, England saw the first stage coach operators running time-tabled public services, changing their horses at specified inns.

Stage coaches started as four-wheeled public coaches, carrying paying passengers and light packages. Each planned journey was determined as far as possible before the need to change horses; a segment or 'stage' was roughly 10 to 15 miles, hence the name.

Coaches were heavy when fully laden and required powerful horses, usually four, though six are suggested as necessary for more difficult journeys.

These new horse-drawn coaches, stage coaches, were not mail coaches; mail coaches developed in the 18th Century.

Horses harnessed to a late 17th Century stage coach ©Doug Eyre

Coaching inns had status higher than ordinary inns, where carriers may well have operated.[18] The White Hart, now called The Lygon Arms, was referred to as a common inn in Broadway, setting it aside from a coaching Inn.[19]

Disregarding the previously mentioned royal patent for the short route between Edinburgh and Leith in 1610, the first stage coach service was London and Chester, the main port to Ireland. The earliest mention of this Irish route is found in Mercurius Politicus (a republican[20] London magazine[21]) on 9 April 1657.

> *For the convenient accommodation of passengers from and betwixt London and West Chester[22], there is provided several stage-coaches, which go from the George Inn, without Aldersgate, upon every Monday, Wednesday, and Friday — to Coventry in two days, for twenty-five shillings; to Stone in three days, for thirty shillings; and to Chester in four days, for thirty-five shillings; and from thence do return upon the same days, which is performed with much ease to the passengers, having fresh horses once a day.*

Shortly afterwards, around 1657, a surprising second coaching route from London to Aberystwyth (Aberistwith) was organised. Why Aberystwyth is a puzzle, and we do not know who was behind this stage company.

On the face of it, there is little to recommend a journey to a Welsh coastal market town that was not only small but obscure in the 17th

---

18. British History online.
19. Curtis Garfield & Alison Ridley, *The Story of the Lygon Arms*, 1992.
20. From 1653, during the Interregnum, England was under various forms of republican government. The Instrument of Government was replaced in May 1657.
21. The only London newspaper at this time published weekly, from June 1650 to May 1660.
22. Chester was the town from which coaches set off to Holyhead, where ships sailed to Ireland.

Century. But, on the other hand, Worcester and Oxford were anything but obscure, having been vital Royalist strongholds only ten years before the route's opening. Moreover, there were few sizable settlements beyond Worcester; the economic return for this coaching route must have been slim beyond the Worcester stage?

Aberystwyth did, however, have an adequate harbour on a high tide to sail to Ireland.

There seem to be several theories as to why establishing this route might have been important:

From 1657 to 1659, Ireland was an essential destination for Cromwell. He had appointed his 4th son, Henry, Major General of Ireland's forces, in the hope of improving relations between the two countries. However, in 1657 the route via Chester was already available. In addition, whilst increased travel to Ireland may well have been a vision, based on Cromwell's ambition to improve ties, his track record in Ireland, especially at the Siege of Drogheda[23], must indeed have meant this was unlikely to materialise so quickly that a new coaching route was needed?

Cromwell could have considered taking troops to Ireland via this route if necessary. However, when the London to Aberystwyth route was being commissioned, Cromwell had been ill with kidney stones. In September 1658, he died due to complications of malaria and his kidney stone problem. His death is said to have been hastened by the demise of his second daughter Elizabeth in August that year. In my opinion, his sons would not have been focussing their attention on a mere coaching route at that time.

Before the civil war, Worcester was such a significant destination, a historically important centre of religion and trading, dating back to the Mercians. It was so severely damaged that a move could have

---

23. Possibly the most ferocious sacking of a town in Irish history.

been to support its full recovery. However, this still would not explain why the route continued to Aberystwyth. The villages and towns it went through were obscure. Aberystwyth, the site of a significant battle during the civil war, was disgarisoned. Its castle had been demolished by 1647. In 1650 it was described as a miserable market town, its buildings transformed into a confused heap of unnecessary rubbish.[24]

Whilst unproven, this route may have been chosen as a clandestine escape route to Ireland for Charles II. Charles had first-hand experience of how a reign could go badly wrong; his escape after the Battle of Worcester to Shoreham in Sussex was traumatic, etching itself on his consciousness, probably for life. He may well have thought through the consequences, should his reign not proceed well; a clandestine escape route via safe catholic strongholds would have seemed attractive, if not essential. Had he needed to flee, the assumption his enemies might have made would have been that the route he took to Ireland would have been via Chester and not to Aberystwyth, giving him more time to escape.

On the Aberystwyth route, almost all the stops from London: Oxford, Moreton in Marsh, (spelt Mortin), Broadway, Pershore and Worcester were home to staunch royalists; in Broadway and Pershore, it was respectively, members of the Coventry[25] and Savage families. Moreover, Aberystwyth Castle itself had been a royalist stronghold that had fallen to the Parliamentarians.

Beyond the English border, much of the land was isolated, with very few settlements; any escape would be quick to Worcester and slower but discrete to Aberystwyth.

---

24. Aberystwyth - *a photographic history of your town*, Tony Cornish & James Plant, Black Horse Books, 2001.
25. In fact the Savages and the Coventry families were both significant landowners in around Pershore and in Broadway, at the time of the Civil War they were firm Royalists.

The mapmaker John Ogilby[26] Esq (1600-1676) had strong connections to Charles II or his court officials. He organised much of Charles II's coronation procession in 1660. He was later commissioned to survey and produce the first road atlas of England and Wales. He started his 100 maps from 'Aberistwith' to London route. A 2019 dissertation[27] debates whether Ogilby, at the behest of Charles II, was complicit in mapping the route to support a planned clandestine Catholic invasion of England and Wales via Aberystwyth, then on to London, after 1670.

The dissertation discusses the then-secret Treaty of Dover, between England and France, signed 1 June 1670. The treaty required (at an unspecified future date) Charles II to convert to the Roman Catholic Church and supply 60 warships and 4,000 soldiers to support Louis XIV, his French cousin, in his war against the Dutch Republic. Louis was then to give Charles II an annual pension of £230,000 plus an additional amount when he announced his conversion to Catholicism to the English People. Furthermore, 6,000 French troops would be sent to England to assist with any rebellion. The thesis considers whether the 1675 map was commissioned as the first of Ogilby's Road Maps to support this invasion.

My research supports this theory. The Aberystwyth to London route, if the occasion had arisen, would have given the French troops an element of surprise. In addition, Ogilby's 1675 map does not highlight much beyond what might interest marching troops: river crossings, fords, hills. All along the route are safe havens, avoiding

---

26. John Ogilby, a 66-year-old Irishman when he arrived in London, after a colourful career turned to map making, having lost his considerable fortune in the 1641 uprising by Irish Catholics. In London, he found a market for the curious, making grand maps of the world and continents such as Africa, Asia, and America.
27. Chris Saville, 2019, student dissertation for The Open University module A329. The making of Welsh history: *Did John Ogilby complicitly map a route from Aberystwyth to London as part of clandestine plans for a Catholic invasion of England and Wales, at the behest of Charles II?* Page 7.

significant settlements, linking to royalist supporters such as Edmund Waller[28] in Beaconsfield.

Could this coaching route have been commissioned as an escape route 18 years earlier if this theory is correct? By 1675 we know of only six English main routes used; the first map was the route that came through Broadway due to topology. There is a need for more research to tease out the reasons behind a route from London to Aberystwyth, planned around 1657, and implemented by 1660.

When Ogilby surveyed Broadway in 1660 when the Angel was completed, he wrote Broadway is *'a well-built town of 5 furlongs length[29] affording several good inns for accommodation.'* Was he confirming Broadway as a suitable stop on the London to Aberystwyth route, with a mind to it being an escape route? Whatever the reason for this route, it survived as the main coaching route. A later document confirmed that the 1722 route[30] was little changed from the route detailed in the 1675 map on the next page.

The 1722 route from Aberistwith to London 199 Miles, thus reckoned.

From Aberistwith to Riodergowy 28, to Ithon? River 9, to Prestain 13, to Leominster 13, to Bramyard 11, to Worcester 12, to Pershore 9, to Broadway 12, to Mortin in Marsh 7, to Easton 13, to Islip 12, to Wheatly Bridge 8, to Tetworth 4, to Wickham 12, to Beaconfield 5, to Uxbridge 8, to Acton 10, to London 8, which is the Metropolis or principal City.

---

28. An outstanding 17th Century Poet, who sided with the King, and who was involved in a plot to capture London for the King (The Waller Plot). He bought his exile for £10,000 avoiding execution and until pardoned 1651.

29. It is roughly a kilometre from the green to the Elizabethan Houses, in the upper part of the High Street - measured.

30. William Stow: *Remarks on London being an exact survey of the cities of London and Westminster, borough of Southwark, and the suburbs and liberties contiguous to them…. places to which penny post letters and parcels are carried, with lists of fairs and markets… to what inns flying coaches, waggons and carriers come, and the days they go out…. keys, wharfs and plying places on the river Thames… description of the great and cross roads from one city and eminent town to another, in England and Wales… the rates of coachmen[sic], chairmen, carmen and watermen… London,* T Norris and H Tracey, 1722.

One section of John Ogilby's 1675 map: Continuation of y'Road From LONDON to ABERISTWITH plate of Second - Commencing at Islip Com Oxford, and Extending Bramyard com Hereford, Containing 67 miles 1 furlong.

There was a practical reason, not simply good fortune, that the route went via Broadway. It was bound to be a stage given the long pull up Broadway Hill, one of the highest points in the Cotswolds. Rising over 1.7 miles from 656 feet to 912 feet, its incline is said to be 16%.

Thomas Habington wrote in his survey of Worcestershire, 1560 - 1647, of *"Broadway being a towne extended in a streete tedyous in its leangthe, especially in the wynter."*

Although no evidence has been found, it is said, in some conditions, with specific loads, tackling Broadway Hill required 17 horses.

July 1752, almost a hundred years after the Angel was built, when more than one company was running stage coaches through Broadway and carriers were run from the White Hart (Lygon Arms), a social regulation was introduced *'that every waggon and other carriage drawn up from the signe of the White Hart, Broadway, to the top of the hill, so far as in the County of Worcester, may be drawn with ten horses if the owner thinks proper.'* [31]

The introduction of coaching would have proven to be more than advantageous to the village; it would have been a lifeline; Broadway's economy depended on the wool trade, a declining industry at the end of the 16th Century.

Sheep rearing was becoming focussed on meat production for England's domestic, urban market. Increasingly Smithfield drovers, with their breeches buttoned at the knees, striped stockings, neat shoes, and short spats[32] would be receiving sheep, though the most spectacular part of the droving trade was concerned with cattle.[33] Additionally, the more delicate 'fluffy' wool from the Iberian

---

31. Worcester Quarter Sessions.
32. W.H. Payne: *The costume of Great Britain* 1804, printed for William Miller, by William Bulmer & Co.
33. Shirley Toulson: *The Drovers*, Shire Books, 2005.

Peninsula's merino sheep had overtaken the sturdy and worsted Cotswold yarn in popularity. The increasing size of European flocks had dramatically reduced England's exports.

Then, new materials such as linen and cotton started to come into England from the New World, adding to the decline in the value of wool.

Chapter 4
Why decide to build a new Inn in Broadway? Why not adapt the White Hart?
1657

Around 1657, when Broadway was identified as a suitable and necessary stage for coaching, and the main thoroughfare, Broadway Street, was a place where services and accommodation would be needed, the leading inn in the village was the White Hart (now The Lygon Arms).

Given the White Hart's prominent position, mid-point on Broadway Street, and its makeover in 1620, which was a significant investment, enlargement, and upgrade by its then-new owner John Treavis, the question that arises is why was this establishment not chosen to provide accommodation and stabling for this stage?

The White Hart was renovated and extended in 1620 to be a four-storey building

The curtilage of the White Hart, though less than the 9 acres of today, was certainly large enough. Its stabling was sufficient. In 1657, it provided horses for post boys and had a carrier business. Both armies had passed through Broadway during the Civil War at different times. The landlady of White Hart, Ursula Treavis, had accommodated, with some discretion, both leaders, Cromwell and Charles I. Many records detail the movements around Broadway during the Civil War; too many to reference in this book. These references[34] leave an impression that as the parliamentarians were scouting to the east of Broadway, the royalists were sneaking across Broadway Hill to the west.

An analysis of the provision of accommodation at the White Hart around 1657 raises a query about the number of serviceable bedrooms available. Although there seem to be ten functional bedrooms, two or three would have been taken up by family members. Around six or seven appear to have been for travellers.[35] When completed, the Angel also offered six or seven for travellers. This number of rooms is consistent with the number of paying passengers inside a coach in those early days. Later the new building offered two more. It, therefore, remains curious that the White Hart did not become the inn of choice when decisions were being made.

In 1654, the White Hart's owner, Mathew Treavis, had inherited the property from his father John on his mother's death three years earlier. He and his family lived in London, where his business interests, linked to the Salters Company, were based. He was a merchant of some standing, with a considerable estate and many business responsibilities.[36]

34. Laird *A Topographical and Historical Description of the County of Worcester*, Sherwood, Neely, and Jones, Paternoster Row; and George Cowie and Co. 1814.
35. Curtis Garfield & Alison Ridley, *The Story of the Lygon Arms*, 1992
36. Ibid.

This was the restoration period; in 1660, Charles II returned to London and took up his Whitehall residence. Change in the city was everywhere. Around 1658, Mathew is thought to have acquired interests in tobacco in Virginia. We know Mathew had determined his son John should manage the White Hart, but when John died, management fell to a third party, Phillip Hodges.[37] Perhaps changes in Broadway were insignificant to Mathew, compared with those taking place in London. Alternatively, it is possible the lack of a direct owner, Mathew being engaged in other matters, and only the innkeeper, Phillip Hodges, to negotiate with, was a complication.

By 1657 the core of the White Hart, with low ceilings and dark rooms, was approximately 350 years old, if not older. Despite the upgrade, it was a well-used meeting and hospitality venue. The community used the reception rooms; the White Hart had a tradition of being used by the village for specific functions and meetings, harking back to the days of the Inner Court. There are suggestions[38] that some innkeepers despised the idea of the new-fangled coaches. Maybe Phillip Hodges, the innholder of the White Hart, fell into that category.

The Angel was to be built to new standards. While it reflected some of the architecture of its older sister across the street externally, internally, its main rooms were more extensive, its ceilings higher, doors and passageways wider. In addition, the new inn's functions would be different than those of the older inns in Broadway, having both the facility to accommodate, in some style, the innholder's family and the flexibility to receive a good number of different types of people, of all classes, simultaneously and accommodate them appropriately.

Coaching inns were to have a much higher status than existing common inns; they were purpose-built and much smarter.

---

37. Will of Mathew Treavis.
38. Various documents and text on the history of coaching.

If the reason for the route was in any way linked to a route where properties belonging to loyal Royalist parishes and supporters could be found, the inn's new owners, the Coventry family, had an excellent pedigree.

Whatever the reason, the White Hart was not favoured as the establishment where the coaches would stop.

From 1660 onwards, sheep and coaches would compete for space; the main street was probably much busier and much messier than we see it today.

Coaching now became the new driver for Broadway's economy, again, just as in the period of the dissolution of the monasteries when Sheldon sold off some of his newly acquired lands to meet his debts, a merchant class emerged, one whose wealth depended on coaching and hospitality rather than farming, sheep, and wool.

This was all well and good but the hullabaloo: the horses, the coach drivers, the carriers, later the gigs, the guards, the passengers, the luggage, the ostlers[39], curious bystanders, manure, smell, noise, dust, dirt, mud in the winter would all part and parcel of this new phenomena; this is the scene that would dominate the village during the next 190 years: day, evenings and sometimes at night. One suspects that the change and its impact crept up slowly on the community, too slowly to resist. On the other hand, historically, Broadway was a community used to constant commotion: the sheep, the urine collection for tucking,[40] drain smells linked to dyeing, the markets, the waggons and carts related to agricultural activities, and drain odours down the High Street, where open streams ran until the late 19th Century.

---

39. Someone who takes car of people's horses.
40. Wool softening, removing of oils, thickening, and strengthening – replaced by fuller's earth.

In 1660, when John Ogilvy wrote of Broadway as *'a well-built town of 5 furlongs length*[41] *affording several good inns for accommodation,'* it is probable that the Angel, though newly completed, was already up and running.

What of other inns around the time of the decision to make Broadway a stage, 1657-9? The Crown and Trumpet, or Trumpet, a much smaller establishment, has existed since the early 17th Century. It does not seem to have been an inn until around 1840 or slightly before. Ivy House,[42] a 14th and 15th Century property, is thought to have been a farmhouse with a smithy in 1660. It bears the date 1574 on one of its doors. It is possible the old Abbot's Grange offered accommodation after the dissolution of the Evesham and Pershore Abbey. Russell House, the site of the original Swan Inn, does not seem to have been built until very early in the 18th Century.[43] The name and licence later moved to two cottages across the road around 1791. They were later extended to create the building we see today. The old Swan was then significantly redesigned to become a gentleman's residence.

Ogilby's reference *'affording several good inns'* must have meant the new Angel Inn, the White Hart and a few outlying smaller inns established when Elizabeth I passed edicts to encourage inns to come forward in a pattern, a few miles between each inn to reduce crime and increase safe journeying, to benefit the economy of the county.

---

41. It is roughly a kilometre from the Green to the Elizabethan houses, Broadway, measured.
42. Broadway Hotel.
43. There is a reference to the Swan Inn in a 1727 Court Leet.

Chapter 5
The Angel Inn, the external building, its construction 1659-1660, additions, new extensions, and renovations

The Angel 2021, the original building 1660 building and a renovated extension 1910

From 1657 onwards, coaching was to play its part in the heightened vision and ambition pervading England. Regardless of a national lack of infrastructure, purpose-built inns began to spring up all around the country.

In the previous chapter, we noted that in Broadway, the Angel, a new purpose-built coaching inn, had been commissioned to serve the Broadway to Moreton in Marsh stage rather than an exiting inn in the village. This chapter will look at the external building and its ownership.

Sources confirm and explain the background to the landowner and commissioner of the Angel being the right honourable Thomas, 2nd

Lord Coventry, Baron of Aylesborough (1606 -1661).[44] In 1660 he already owned the property next door to the east of the Angel, which included outbuildings and stables.

His father, Thomas Coventry (1578-1640), was born at Croome D'Abitot, Worcestershire, educated at Balliol College, Oxford, 1592 to 1594. Known for his exceptional legal abilities, sound and sterling qualities, he was an influential figure in parliament before the many protectorate parliaments. However, it was not until Charles I was crowned, in 1625, that Thomas received his titles, the recognition for his hard work that he had sought all his life. In 1625 he was made Lord Keeper of the Great Seal; in this capacity, he delivered Charles I 's reprimand to the Commons on 9 March 1626. Then, on 10 April 1628, he received the title of Baron Coventry of Aylesborough in Worcestershire. His stewardship and abilities enabled him to amass a fortune, particularly during his years as Lord Keeper of the Great Seal.

Like many successful and professional men of his day, he had been keen to purchase land and a country estate. The Coventry's understood land and property underpinned status and power; this encouraged him to extend his ownerships. As early as 1627, as part of this plan, he acquired land and tithes[45] in Broadway from the largest landowner in the village, Walter Savage, the owner of Broadway's Greate Farm.

These lands were later settled on his eldest son, from his first marriage to Sarah Sebright, in 1627[46] when he, Thomas, 2nd Lord Coventry, Baron of Aylesborough (1606 -1661), came of age and married Mary Craven. In 1625, Thomas 2nd Lord Coventry, at the age of twenty, had been elected Member of Parliament for Droitwich. In 1628 he was elected MP for Worcestershire and sat until 1629

---

44. The Coventry family connection is confirmed in the will of the first innholder John Phipps, 1673.
45. These would be converted to land after the Inclosure Act of 1771.
46. Catherine Gordon: *The Coventrys of Croome*, Phillimore & Co. Ltd, 2000.

when King Charles decided to rule without parliament for eleven years. Thomas 2nd Lord Coventry supported the Royalist cause in the English Civil War, defending Worcester in 1642 against the Parliamentary Army, led by Sandys, despite making peace with Parliament in October 1642. He paid heavily for his involvement. In 1643, he was permitted to go abroad on health grounds. However, his money and goods in the East India Company assets were frozen on 15 January 1644. On 20 September the same year, the House of Lords assessed his fines at £1,500, leading to all his goods and chattels in his Westminster house being seized; on 11 April 1645, they were inventoried and sold to pay his fine. In addition, he was suspected of having Royalist sympathies in 1651 and supporting Charles II when he was in France. Though cleared of the charges, he was imprisoned for a period in 1655.[47]

He was alive to the dawn of a new era after the Civil War. Like his father, he was willing to invest in ventures like the Angel. And he needed to recover some of his losses during the Civil War. The Angel's purpose now was to accrue profit to its owner through the lease of land and property. The innholder, in turn, would make his income from the provision of accommodation, food, stabling for horses and replacement mounts.

The Coventry's connection with the Angel and its lands is confirmed in several ways:

- the will of John Phipps, the first innholder of the Angel, who died in 1673, establishes the inn was leased for 99 years from Thomas, 2nd Lord Coventry.

- some years later, the will of a philanthropic farmer,[48] in Broadway, Thomas Hodges, dated 1686, referred to the

47. Glyn Redworth /Ben Coates: *The History of Parliament* Volumes: 1604-1629 also *Coll. of State Papers of John Thurloe* ed. T. Birch, iii. 593.
48. After the dissolution of the monasteries, 1539, the Crown's sale of Church lands to Babington, and his sale to Daston and Sheldon, Sheldon was over stretched. His sale of land

promise of a Free School to be set up by Lady Coventry. The school was to be free for the poor of the parish. If Lady Coventry were to provide the school, as he thought according to his will, would create a Trust to sustain the poor boys with funds to purchase their apprenticeships, tools, clothing, including uniforms and shoes, or boots. Hodge's seventy-five [49] acres, termed school land, was put in Trust until his wife died. Part of the land to the east of the Angel was school land, a small part of which was used to build Broadway's National School in 1855. Part of the Coventry land became a playground for the school in 1855.

- In 1771, an award map, the product of the Inclosure[50] Act's Inquiry into the Manor of Broadway, drafted to clarify land ownership identified the land and buildings next to the Angel as being owned by the right honourable George William Coventry, 6th Earl of Coventry (1722-1809). [51] [52]

The Angel's ownership, by the Coventry family, explains its quality design and build; the finest limestone masonry unit, rectangular cuboid, precisely cut on all faces, was used in its construction.

---

to local Freeman created a new middle class. These newly wealthy merchants and farmers often embraced philanthropy. Hodges set out to support a new charitable school being set up, by Lady Coventry.

49 When investigated by the Inclosure Act Commissioners 1771 it was 62 acres, some had gone missing.

50. The Inclosure Act, dealt with enclosures of land. Its common now to see it spelt enclosure.

51. The key on the 1771 award map identifies C as the Right Honourable George William Coventry, 6th Earl of Coventry, MP for Worcestershire from 1747 to 1751. When his father died, he joined the House of Lords. It was George who restored the Neo-Palladian Croome Court at Croome d' Abitot, between 1754-1760.

52. Coventry is thought to have stabled coach horses at this property to facilitate his coaches travelling to London. He may have kept horses for riding with the Cotswold Hunt (West of Stow towards Cheltenham and north towards Broadway) from 1772. History of the Cotswold Hunt. www.cotswoldhunt.co.uk.

The build dates are carved onto commemorative shields on the front bay windows' parapet; the build start date of 1659 is to the east, and the completion date 1660 is to the west. A third middle shield bears the letter P, which could reflect the surname of the first innholder John Phipps?

Commemorative shields, now very weather-worn, above the central bay

The Angel is a generous four-storied building, three main storeys and one storey within a section of its slate roof. Its triple-gabled frontage, mullioned windows, and emphasised centralised bay windows, bearing similarities to the 1620 frontage of the White Hart (Lygon Arms), give the building its dominating, slightly Gothic overtones. However, the back of the Angel is of a more practical, simpler construction.

The imposing four-storey building

Both buildings, the Angel and the White Hart have exuberant ball finials more familiar in buildings of a later period.

A delightful and possibly 17th Century feature of the building is the leaded mullioned windows, now only visible on the second floor. In addition, the high-pointed two-light dormer windows have original period glass and lead fitted casements, not necessarily the original windows of the Inn.

A second-floor front window

Evidence,[53] 1771, confirms in the late 18th Century, coaches approached the inn's yard via Keytes Lane; passengers alighting from a coach would have entered the Angel through its large, heavily hinged and bolted rear door leading into its kitchen and little parlour.

The well at the rear of the building, in the neighbouring garden, is now ornamental. Many of Broadway's more significant properties in the 17th Century had wells; villagers took water from the open streams along the street. This well would have provided an abundance of spring water for drinking and watering the horses in the yard.

Family, friends, and their prestigious freeholder, Lord Coventry himself, could have used the semi-circular stone steps to enter the inn via the door on the street (High Street).

53. The 1771 Inclosure Act map of Broadway Street.

An inventory taken on 17th February 1673 mentions new rooms and areas added to the Angel after 1660: the new room, new hall, and new cellar…..

The 1664-1665 entry in the Worcestershire Hearth Tax Register,[54] which recorded, for that year, all the houses in the County of Worcester that had thirteen to nineteen hearths, confirms there was a newly built extension added between 1660 and 1664. The Angel, in the hands of John Phipps, has twelve hearths plus a furnace in the brewhouse. Given the 1660 build had only ten hearths, three must have been in this new extension.

Today, we can still see the six gable chimneys in the original 1660 building, with diagonal shafts, cornices, and lozenge friezes. There are three to the east, two located centrally, at the rear of the building, and one to the west.

Nine of the thirteen hearths can be traced to the original building. The three chimneys to the east served three floors:

---

54. The Hearth Tax was introduced in 1662 and collected twice a year until Lady Day in 1689. It provided names only in the years 1662-6 and 1669-74.

- the kitchen and the little parlour hearths on the ground floor, now the Cabinet of Curiosity room and part of the corridor; only one remains,

- the room above the kitchen on the first floor, now the Broadway Colony Room - two hearths are confirmed on a first-floor layout dated 1907,

- two fireplaces to the east on the second floor, the Museum's special exhibition area. A 2012 layout and photographs show that one fireplace to the east is behind a plasterboard.

The two chimneys to the rear served the Great Parlour on the ground floor and the Great Chamber on the first floor, so named in the 1673 will and inventory. These are the Museum's largest rooms.

The chimney to the west served only the second floor with two fireplaces, although now one has been removed. This area on the second floor is now the Museum's education room. No further blocked fireplaces have been found.

The tenth hearth was the furnace for the brewhouse.

Therefore, to arrive at the figure of thirteen, there must have been chimneys and fireplaces in the new building. The inventory of 1673 is clear; it says *'new hall with hearth, new room with hearth, and gatehouse room with hearth.'*

It, therefore, seems likely that as stage coaching took off, some of the deficiencies in the original 1659 design became apparent. It is feasible the original planners and architects of the building underestimated the needs of the coachmen or how successful, despite the odds, stage coaching would become. Coaches were built for six passengers, eight at a push, but soon accommodated more.

It was not until the mid 19th Century that there were any significant external changes to the building; they came about due to new uses. Later chapters will take the reader through the many different owners and tenants from when the Inn appears to have ceased being an Inn to today. The 1771 map of Broadway Street shows the 1660-1664 new building initially extended to the footpath, later known as Broad Close Lane (now a right of way), to the west.

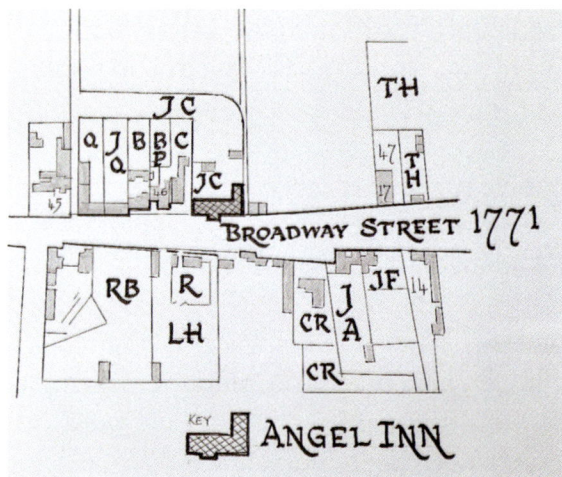

A reproduction of the 1771 Broadway Inclosure Act, award map showing the Angel in the Estate of JC, John Cormell, ©Doug Eyre

A 20th Century aerial photograph showing left to right, the 1855 National School, the Crown, and the Angel sites, reflecting many of the 1771 map features

The section of the award map from Keytes Lane, near Leamington Road almost to Kennel Lane, shows the Angel's buildings extended as far as the ancient footpath. There is a structure on the site of the current Millennium Gardens and buildings to the rear of the Angel, possibly the brewhouse, barns or additional stabling. The long wall of the neighbouring property to the east, The Crown, helps create an enclosed yard for the Angel.

The access to the Angel's yard is marked JC. Its width suggests that, in 1771, stage coaches used this route rather than stop on the street.

The external appearance of the new building is intriguing; what we see today was designed in 1910 for modern living and the motor car, not stage coaches. A sketch, with an almost illegible date possibly, 1822 or 1823, found amongst Tudor House papers used by the Ashmolean project manager to research the building before the Museum opened, proposes a design for this new extension which for several reasons, seems to be a fair representation of the original extension.

The date of the drawing could be at anytime between 1696 and 1851 as the front elevation shows that twenty-six windows are blocked up, indicating the building, when sketched, was subject to the window tax.[55][56] It is unlikely the windows were blocked up when the Inn was fully functioning, which narrows down the date of the drawing to the hundred years between, say 1771 when the Inn was part of the Cormell Trust and 1851 when the window tax was lifted. Drawn on the front step and by the door, the milk churns, used for transporting

55. The window tax was implemented by William III to recoup losses due to coin chippings. It lasted 156 years and was repealed 24 July 1856. It was a banded tax, for example in 1747 for a house with ten to fourteen windows the tax stood at 6d per window. Fifteen to nineteen windows it stood at 9p exceeding twenty or more 1s per window. The tax was raised six times between 1747 and 1808.
56. https://Historyhouse.co.uk/articles/window_tax.html

milk rather than churning, help us date the sketch to around 1850,[57] if not shortly before.

An early sketch, date not legible, possibly 1820-1850 of the Angel, Tudor House, suggests the possible structure of the new building, added between 1660 and 1664

The sketch gives clues to the possibility that the new building was part wood and stone; this sizeable barn-like structure, with substantial, hinged, wooden gates, would have incorporated the rooms mentioned in the inventory. The gatehouse chamber possibly accommodated the coachman. The west end room could have been well placed near the stables to house the ostler.[58] A new room could have accommodated the linen store and possibly an additional

---

57. Milk was delivered in wooden barrel like churns, these were replaced by galvanised milk churns from the 1850s. https://www.igg.org.uk/gansg/12-linind/milk.html
58. The man who looked after the individual horses of or team when the coach or guests arrived.

servant. The new hall could have been helpful for functions. An entrance to the yard from the street in 1660, with large wooden gates, would not have seemed out of place. The new building added before 1664[59], too, could have incorporated a passage to the rear, even a haulway. A rear entrance would have been perhaps more accommodating by the early 18th Century as seating on the roof of stage coaches had replaced the domed or flat-roofed coaches of earlier years.

The 1673 inventory talks of a new cellar; its arch is still visible today, suggesting the rear wall of the new building was, in part, Cotswold stone. From a security perspective, it is reasonable to propose there was a stone wall between the public path and the stables.

Another photograph dated 1858 entitled 'the Old House Broadway` gives some credence to the sketch; several elements are consistent, but others such as the door to the east, on the ground floor, possibly the door into a little parlour do not.

The main building looks the same in this 1858 photograph though now only eleven of the windows are blocked up; they remain despite the window tax having been repealed; the cost of replacing the blocked windows would have been a considerable outlay. It may have been spread over a few years.

The photograph confirms that the new building to the west is still in place but hints that the degree of dilapidation is worsening. 1820-1858 is known to have been a period of rolling tenancies; these are set out in a subsequent chapter. It is likely the fabric of the building suffered at this time. Today, we note only the rear dormer to the east has been removed; presumably, it too fell into disrepair in the mid 19th Century.

---

59. 1664 record of the hearth 13 and the inventory 1673 referred to the new buildings, new room, new hall. .

An old house in Broadway previously belonging to ....Cotterill now 1858 to Stephen Averill

Yet another photograph, dated 1880–1882, reveals that between 1856 and 1880-1882, the original old extension had undergone a traumatic change. The two-storey new building, including the new hall, the gatehouse chamber, and the new room with linen store, do not appear to have survived. The extension is revealed to be much reduced and sits behind a long buttress wall, incorporating a substantial wooden gate. An 1880 map confirms this situation.

George Hudson on the steps of Tudor House, circa 1882. The large buttress wall to the right appears to be supporting the whole wall of the original building.

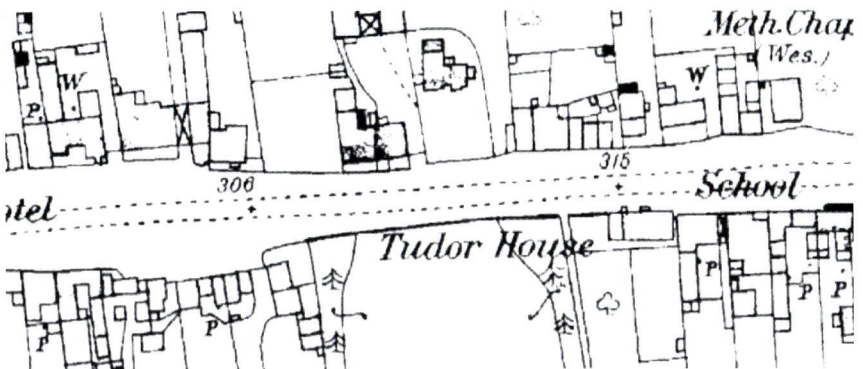

Tudor House around 1880 showing a significantly reduced extension behind the wall

This much-reduced extension is reflected in the sketch attached to deeds from 1881 to 1907.

This situation did not last long. Photographs dated between 1885 and 1887 show that a new owner rebuilt and updated the property by adding a solid extension, including a haulway to the east of the rebuild. The rebuild was in stone, a change of material that could indicate fire had been a factor in 1881; however, fire reddens Cotswold stone, and there are no visibly fired damaged stones. So, it's not known what caused this loss of buildings: storm, flood[60] fire or just neglect?

Layouts dated 1907 confirm both the ground and first floor, internal layout of the main building and the 1885-7 extension.

An early photograph circa 1900 showing a rebuilt extension – archway to the east

---

60. The building would have been flooded from the springs, the brook and run off in the many recorded flood incidences in Broadway over the years.

The old 1887 haulway is still visible today from the rear of the property.

The eastern archway, the old haulway, seen from the rear of the building 2020

Finally, layouts drawn up in 1910 resulted in a complete refurbishment of the extension, greatly improving its layout, and setting to rights some building changes that had occurred during the various tenancies. Now we see the haulway is changed from the rustic door set in a large arch to the east of the new building to an altogether more pleasing, more elegant archway to the west, which facilitated access to the motor car, then a '*new-fangled*' way of travelling.

The extension today shows the archway relocated to the west

In 1664, in the County of Worcester,[61] there were only thirty-one houses within all the County's village settlements, in twenty-seven communities, that were large enough to feature on the Hearth Register; therefore, this Register is also a record of the relative wealth of significant families living in those named communities.

Only two Broadway properties were recorded:

Broadway Court, Broadway's Greate Farm, on Le Bury Stret,[62] demolished, apart from its gatehouse to the stables around 1733-1774. This building had 16 hearths and was part of the estate of Walter Savage Esq (1628 - 1706).

The other was the Angel Inn, property of John Phipps.

---

61. Now part of Worcestershire.
62. Now called Snowshill Road.

Whereas the White Hart Inn had evolved from ecclesiastical roots, the Angel was founded solely on private investment, underlining the Inn's build as an exciting venture capital opportunity in today's parlance.

Chapter 6
The Innholder and his family,
1660-1676

John Phipps's will and inventory, dated 1673 and Thomasyn his wife's will and inventory, dated 1676 and 1677, respectively, enables the reader to learn more about the family living and running the Angel before moving on to look at the internal layout of the inn.

The layout of the Angel internally accommodated the passenger, the paid servants, stable hands, the innholder and his family. Before the chapters take us inside the inn, knowing more about this family helps us understand why the Great Parlour and Great Chamber were not initially public rooms.

Researching the family was difficult; they were not a significant family in terms of records. Inconveniently, Phipps's name was not uncommon in Worcestershire, Berkshire, and Shropshire. In the 17th Century, there were two families of that surname in Broadway alone that were likely to be related somehow. A fair representation has been achieved using parish records and the wills.

No evidence has been found to date that this family was linked in any way to Sir William Phips, or Phipps (1651-1695), the first native of New England to be knighted, after which Pittsburgh is said to be named. Nor can I find links to the Worcester family of Phipps. Moreover, any suggestion that John Phipps' father was married to Elizabeth Neighbour has been discounted. There are too many discrepancies in the names of the children.

Born in 1607, John Phipps, the Innholder of the Angel, was the son of John Phipps of Broadway. Few records exist regarding his mother or father. However, the Parish records John's marriage to Thomasyn[63], of Broadway also born in 1607. They had seven children, four boys: John, Francis, Edward, and William and three girls: Frances, Elizabeth, and Ann.

When John, senior at the age of 53, and his wife Thomasyn took up the role of Innholder in 1660, it is thought all his children, except for John 23, accompanied their parents: Edward was around 20, Francis 18, and William 4. Elizabeth was 22, Frances 18, and Anne 8. Therefore, the largest rooms at the Inn appear to have been the family rooms; their family size of eight, two adults and six children probably necessitated this.

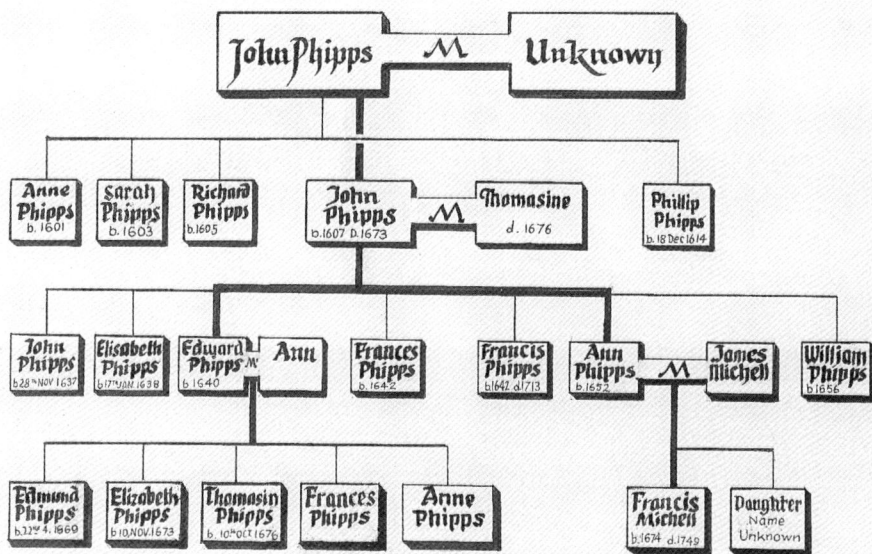

The family tree of John Phipps, Innholder of the Angel, 1660- 1673, Broadway, based on parish records and wills, ©Doug Eyre

---

63. Sometimes spelt Thomasine.

No further record has been found of their son John, who was the only child not mentioned in John Phipps will dated 1673. Possibly there had been a severing of connections due to family issues. He may have died, or perhaps he was one of the numerous young people seeking adventure and success beyond England in the new Americas, and the family had lost contact with him?

Around this period, a Broadway Phipps family has been traced to Broadwell, but links back to John and Tomasyn have not been proven.

Who organised or how John Phipps came to take up the lease of the building, and become Innholder at the age of 53, is unknown? To have his initial P on the middle shield above the central bay window[64] suggests he was involved with the commissioning and possibly the design of the Inn. There may have been a connection with the building owner or another member of the Coventry family. Curiously, a John Phipps 1747-1752, working for the Coventry family, created the serpentine lake at Croome Court. He may have descended from the Phipps of Broadway connection, but the link has not yet been proven.

When John died, aged 66, thirteen years after taking up his position as an innholder, his will of January 8, 1673, confirmed he was weak and sick, but of sound mind, and that only his wife, Thomasyn and their son William, a minor, were living at the Inn. Sons Edward, and Francis, daughters Elizabeth, Frances, and Ann, may well have assisted him and their mother in the running of the Inn, but they were no longer domiciled at the Inn.

Edward was married. John and Thomasyn's first grandchild, Edmund, was born around April 1669.[65] Edward and his wife had three

---

64. See explanation on page 38.
65. Early parish records were linked to the Church and concern themselves with baptism dates not birth dates.

daughters: Frances, Ann, and Elizabeth, born in November 1673. Unfortunately, we do not have records for the baptism[66] of Frances or Ann. Edward's fourth daughter was born just before Thomasyn's death in 1676 and was named after her grandmother.

John's daughter Ann, in 1672, married James Michell.[67] They had two children, including a son named Francis after his uncle. This son would grow up working closely with his uncle, inherit the Inn, and eventually take up his reigns to run or oversee the Inn from 1714 to 1749.

John Phipps's will not only throws light on his role as innholder but additionally sets out the extent of his estate, gives us the names of his family members, and the legal arrangement between himself and the Inn's freeholder. John had purchased a lease for four score and nineteen years (ninety-nine years). The freeholder at the time of John's death in 1673 would have been George Coventry, 3rd Baron Coventry (1628- 1680), the eldest son of Thomas Coventry, 2nd Baron Coventry and Mary Craven.

John's will records the Angel, [68] was bequeathed to Thomasyn, with all barns, stables, outhouses, buildings, backside (land behind), and garden,[69] ground, adjoining and belonging to, plus an estimated twenty-five acres of arable land in the common fields of Broadway. The lease for the remaining term passed to his wife, giving her the benefits of any profits and advantages from the Inn, its outbuildings, grounds, and the 25 acres already being worked.

---

66. Ibid.
67. Sometimes spelt Mitchel or Mitchell.
68. In the will the Angel is spelt with a double ll.
69. Gardens in the 17th Century were not as a garden today they provided everything needed for eating or health – a good example is the National Trust Garden at Culross Palace in Scotland.

In addition, Thomasyn benefited from all the messuage [70] and tenements in Broadway that were in John's possession or occupation adjoining the Angel. This was land and property John had recently purchased from Henry, Farmer Esq. of Rushmore, in the County of Oxon, that was formerly in the occupation of Edmund Turner.

On Thomasyn's death, according to John's will, this land, which Edward was managing, would pass to Edward, providing that within six months of his mother's death, he paid his brother upon his inheritance Francis £100. Until the £100 sum was paid, Francis was to have the use of these lands and tenements. The term 'use' is thought to have meant the income thereof.

Furthermore, the will specified that on his mother's death, Francis was to receive all the Broadway tenements,[71] originally owned by his father, purchased from John Priest but at the time of John's death, were also in Edward's possession.

The will implies that even when John and Thomasyn were running the Inn with the help of Francis and perhaps their daughters, Edward managed the families' landholdings. Edward was already supporting a family, and his father's legacy would enable him and his heirs to be independent of the running of the Inn.

Francis was also adequately provided for, with sufficient income to buffer the 'cash flow' challenges incumbent with the management of an Inn, and indeed a longer-term buffer.

Innkeeping certainly seems to have provided John Phipps with sufficient profits to buy additional land, which he purchased outright. However, an Inn running profitably was not always to be the case. We have no insight into the arrangements concerning the business, the early choice of this route, or the lease coming from the

---

70. A dwelling house with outbuildings and land assigned to its use.
71. Assumed land not adjacent to the inn.

Coventry's, but all suggest the impetus for the venture was better links to the Capital.

William is mentioned explicitly in the will in a way that implies he was still a minor, under the age of 21, and would eventually be provided for through his mother's inheritance. As previously stated, son John is not mentioned.

Son Edward or his grandchild Edmund[72] Phipps, Edward's son (only 4), receives John Phipps household items[73] and furniture in the Great Hall (often called Great Parlour) and the Great Chamber[74] over the Hall. These items had been purchased from Mr Henry Farmer and probably added to over the years.

John left ten shillings to his daughter-in-law, Ann, Edwards's wife, to buy herself a ring, and six shillings, and eight pence to each of Edwards daughters living: Frances, Ann and Elizabeth Phipps.

His will makes no mention of any legacy to his daughters. Elizabeth, Frances, and Ann aged 35, 31 and 21, respectively. This lack of a gift or small inheritance may imply that all three of his daughters were married by the date of John's death in 1673. However, only the marriage of Ann, the youngest, has been confirmed in parish records.

Son Francis and his mother Thomasyn were the executors of the 1673 will.

---

72. Spellings were often lax; Edmund might be used for Edward.
73. Referred to as stuffe.
74. The Great Hall and Great Chamber are descriptions in the will, The Great Parlour is the description for the Great Hall in the inventory, these are now Broadway Museum's Room 3 and Room 5.

Chapter 7
The internal layout of The Angel Inn and its extensions over the Centuries
1660 -1910

The previous chapter looked at ownership of the Inn and external aspects of the main 1660 building and the new extension, which was added shortly after the original, sometime between 1660 and 1664.

We have established, not immediately but probably as soon as coaches carried passengers on the roof, many more passengers than initially envisaged needed to be accommodated. As discussed, passengers likely entered the building from the yard through its substantial rear door, with its heavy period locks. They would have been welcomed into the warm kitchen, with its range, blue lias stone flagged floor and 17th Century staircase leading to the bedchambers.

They must have been impressed with the building internally; the elegant fireplaces, large light rooms, charming window designs set in stone mullions would have been more than expected in a provincial village, such as Broadway.

Using two inventories, John Phipps in February 1673 and his wife, Thomasyn's in 1677, this chapter seeks to tease the layout of the Angel internally in 1673 and note internal changes over the years in either the main building or extension. Unfortunately, we have no actual layouts until 1907. A further chapter will look at the contents of each room.

The names of the rooms[75] in the following layouts are based on the detailed inventory of John Phipps possessions in 1673.

---

75. Detailed in the Inventory 1673 and a second inventory 1676

In addition, the location of the rooms is influenced by the order in which the three scribes documented the rooms.

There are no layouts for the new building, but the inventory room names imply two storeys. The layout (page 62) incorporates the previously mentioned sketch, 1820-1823.

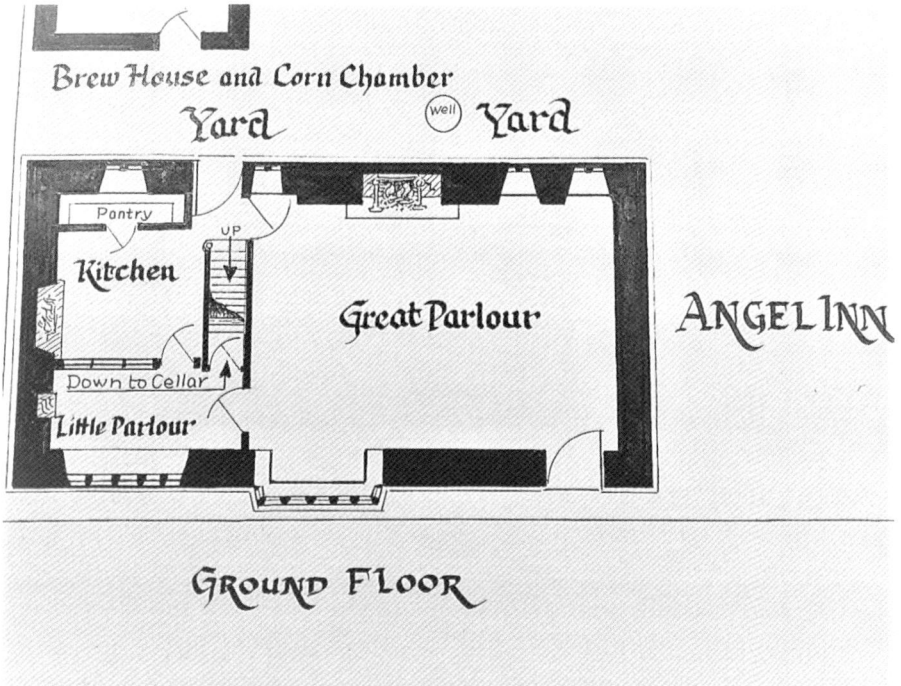

Ground Floor, 1673. Original Building, 1660, ©Doug Eyre

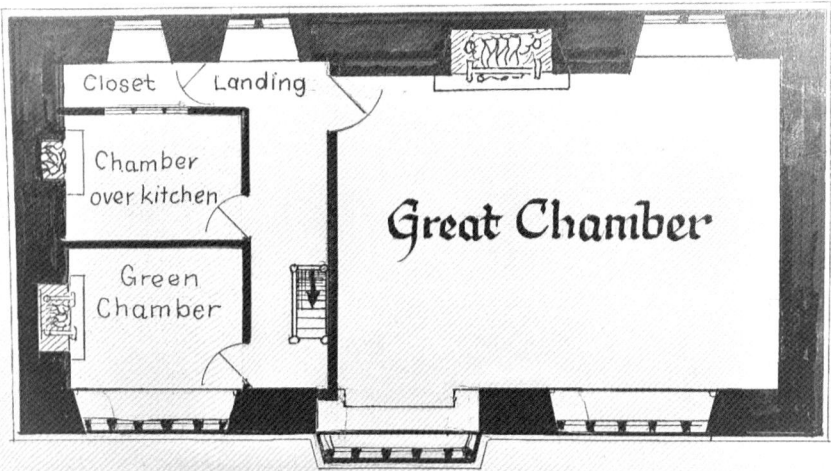

First Floor, 1673, Original Building, 1660, ©Doug Eyre

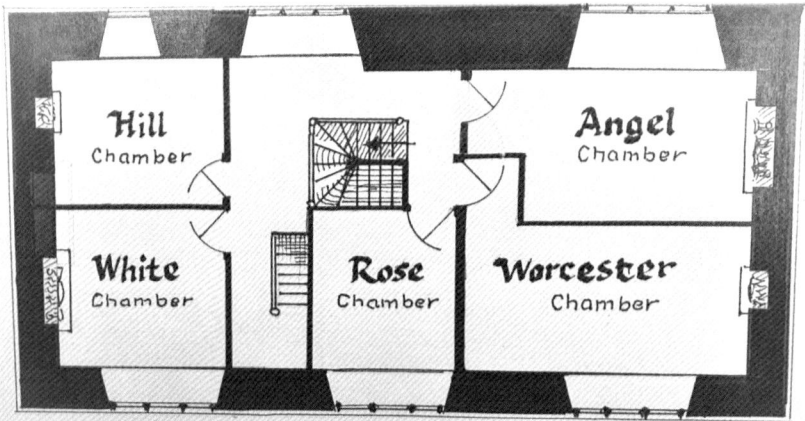

Second Floor, 1673, Original Building, 1660 ©Doug Eyre

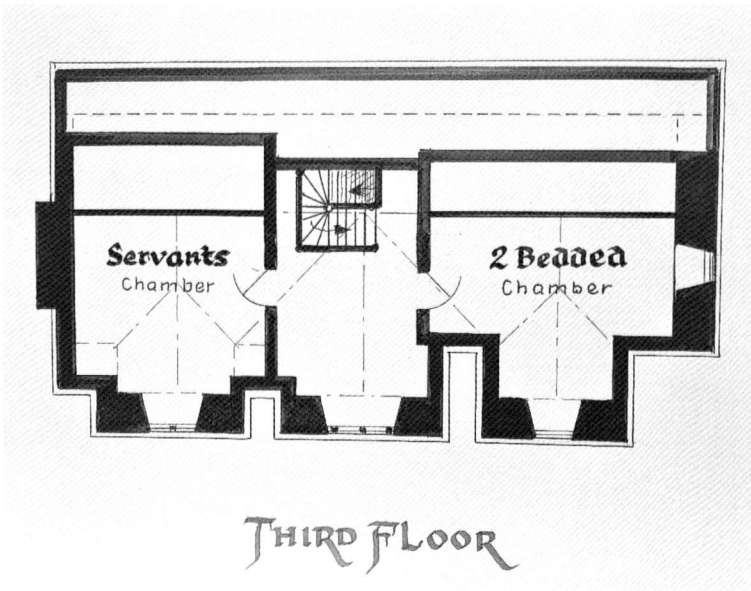

The rooms in the roof on the third-floor original building 1660, ©Doug Eyre

EXTENSION

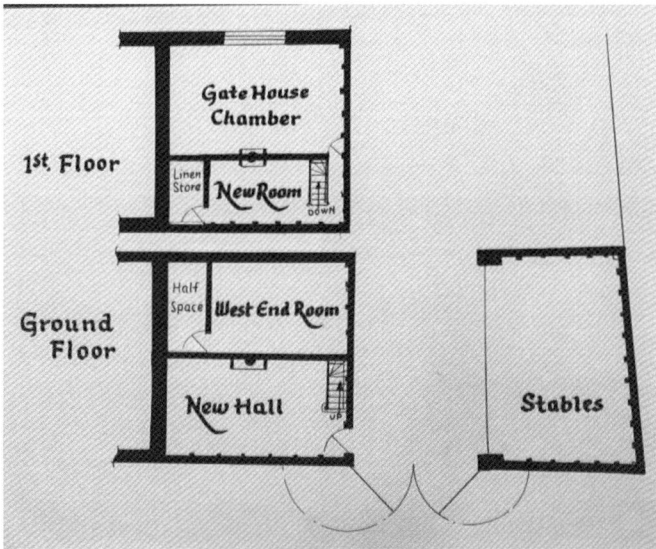

A possible layout of the new buildings built added between 1660 and 1664-5, ©Doug Eyre

In the main building post-1673, some of the internal changes over the years have been:

- the collapse of one of the rear dormers on the second floor,
- window changes due to the window tax,
- the removal of some fireplaces,
- doors created to join the main building and the extension on the ground and first floor,
- The addition of a second rough staircase within the Great Parlour, then its removal.
- the addition of a new staircase between the ground and first floor,
- the addition of a water closet,
- partitioning in the old kitchen,
- the addition of panelling in the 20th Century,
- the addition of antique ironwork and window glass,
- doorways into an extension.
- the recent acquisition of a new kitchen.

The building age stretches over so many centuries that lighting, heating, and piping must have changed frequently.

In the Great Parlour, judging from the timbers in the northwest corner, a section of the wall between it and the hall appears to have been removed to considerably widen the access at some point in its coaching history. This change correlates to that period when there were more passengers on coaches. They could have entered from Broadway Street, almost falling into the Parlour's offer of warmth and comfort in the winter and a quiet, cool refuge from the malodorous street in the summer months.

Once the family no longer ran the Inn from the mid-18th Century, it is most likely that the family rooms, the Great Parlour and the Great Chamber were used differently. The Great Parlour would have been a busy reception room meeting the many needs of the passengers:

eating a hasty meal of variable quality, having a haircut or shave, replacing some provision, resting, changing wet apparel. According to the 1677 inventory, the Great Chamber had become a communal bed chamber for at least five passengers; it is likely for those who could not afford a private room.

Considering the internal layout of the extension, we are somewhat more fortunate in having some sketches and photographs to assist our understanding. The layout on page 62 proposed a possible original layout of the extension; it's not until 1881 that this extension appears to have reduced significantly. The size reduction was confirmed by the 1881 photograph and an ordinance map of 1880 and by a slight sketch found with a deed covering arrangements 1834 to 1881 and one other deed.

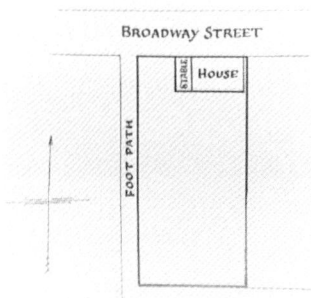

Copy of a sketch of the site of the Angel attached to several documents dated 1834-1882[76]
©Doug Eyre

As stated earlier, a new owner rebuilt the 'missing' extension in 1887. Later chapters, which outline ownership of the Angel after the family to today, will expand further.

In terms of the internal layout, most helpful is one drawn up in 1907 before a major refurbishment took place. Equally valuable is the one after the refurbishment had taken place in 1910.

---

76. The footway to the west is today a public right of way.

1907 and 1910 Layouts

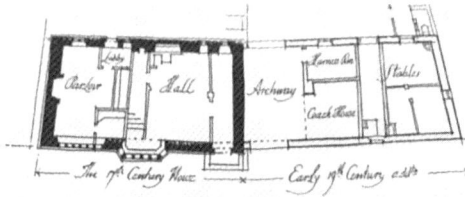

GROUND FLOOR PLAN AS IN 1907.

1907 Ground Floor layout, main building, and extension, before the 1910 restoration

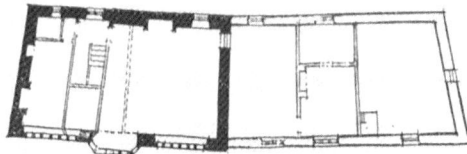

FIRST FLOOR PLAN AS IN 1907.

1907 First Floor layout, main building, and extension before the 1910 restoration

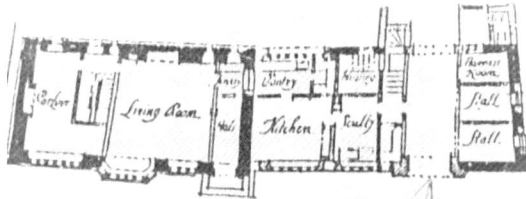

GROUND FLOOR PLAN 1910.

1910 Ground Floor layout, main building, and extension, after C.E. Mallow's restoration

FIRST FLOOR PLAN, 1910.

1910 First Floor layout main building, and extension after C.E. Mallow's restoration

Chapter 8
Details of The Inventory of John Phipps, Innholder of The Angel Inn, 1673

When using any inventory as a source document, it is sensible to remember that the items identified in a specific room in a will at the time of death can be complicated by the legacies referenced in the actual will. If the room contents are specified in the will, family members may move the deceased assets to favour a beneficiary. For example, "I leave the contents of room X to Y" might result in family members moving additional items into room X immediately before an independent inventory is taken.

As was typical for larger estates, on 17 February 1673, three local clerks prepared a complete and detailed probate inventory of John Phipps contents at the Angel. With the rise of the wealthier yeoman class in the 17th Century, inventories were often divided up room by room, as was the inventory of John Phipps.[77] The Inn's assets were valued at the healthy sum of £419 3s 10d. The clerical recorders would have only been interested in John's possessions, not Phipps other assets, lands, tenements, or his wife or family's assets. They would have included items to be inherited after probate. The £419 3s is a goodly sum today in terms of wealth and economic status. In terms of economic power, it would be worth substantially more at the time.

The will, dated 8 January 1673, was finally proven on 21 May 1674.

---

77. Later in the 18th Century in general for most people possessions were too numerous to record and an overall sum was agreed.

Using the descriptions in the probate inventories,[78] it has proven possible to speculate on the internal layout of the Angel in 1673, and how they fitted with the details of the contents of each specifically named room on each floor, almost but not entirely down to the last pair of pot hooks tell us more. When considering the contents of a room, it is also helpful to remember this was a period before separate rooms and the privacy we take for granted today. Pepys is an excellent source of domestic organisation in this period.

The recorders who produced the four-page inventory grouped items as far as possible and declared it the "true and best inventory of all of John Phipps, late of Broadway in the County of Worcester."

Even though not all the items listed were legible, and spelling, secretary hand, and the abbreviations of the period, were a challenge, it is possible to summarise much of the inventory. However, a missing page necessitates the author to use handwritten notes and estimate in some places. The italics are comments on the inventory.

Summary of the Inventory of John Phipps 1673

His (John Phipps) wearing apparel on the date of death and money in his purse £5.00.

Ground Floor

In the Kitchen with Hearth, £27.06s: Thirty-three large dishes of pewter, three dozen and eight pewter plates, ten small dishes of pewter, twenty pewter porringer dishes, nine round pots of pewter, thirteen pewter chamber pots, thirteen pewter flagons, one dozen candlesticks, two pewter pie plates, and a pewter roast plate, ten pewter joint pots, and three pewter wine rests, one dozen of and

---

78. Carried out by Jo Farmer, Thomas Austin, Thomas Wood and one other.

twelve of other items. Five brass pots and one brass pan, four large brass bottles, six small brass bottles, two warming pans, three small brass ladles, two brass and one brass item, five iron spits, two dripping pans, one fork, two gridirons, an iron grate and hooks for the fire, a pair of tongs, one fire shovel, twelve other pieces of tin, three pairs of pot hooks and links, pair of bellows. One table board and frame, one cupboard, three chairs and four stools. Two pairs of bellows and a pair of wooden dishes and everything necessary to a kitchen not yet covered.

In the 17th Century inn, the kitchen, typically one room, was the heart and soul of any inn, warm and inviting. Its shelves were full of pewter, brass, and iron dishes, earthenware mugs, and pewter pitchers. Adjacent would be a common room serving both food and drink, large windows let light into the main rooms, and transom windows brought light into other areas of the Inn such as the parlour.

Pewter Plates   Pewter Flagon

Table boards, which folded, were sat at; it was considered a luxury to have a table that stayed up all the time, forms (benches) or stools were sat on. Occasional, a cut-down barrel would be used as a gaming table.

17th Century Table Board   17th Century Stool

The food served in a 17th/18th Century Inn is well documented. The inn had a good-sized garden, fields, yard, stables, chickens, and pigs. Bread, the staff of life, at the Inn was made with finely ground wheat rather than cheaper grains such as barley and rye. Cheese and eggs played a large part in the diet. Chicken and game birds were to hand. The meat was fresh, often cooked in a stew or pies; salting and spicing helped meat to last longer. The pot was the mainstay of any inn, and there are stories of scurrilous innkeepers offering soup or stew so hot that much had to be left when the passengers had to get back in the coach, done so the innkeeper could put it back in the pot! Pigs were slaughtered in December and preserved to make, amongst other things sausages, and bacon. The pork was used alongside beef, veal, new lamb, hogget, or mouton. Fish was rare and had to be fresh.[79] Vegetables included peas, beans, asparagus, cabbage, root vegetables, salad, spinach, leeks, and cauliflower; some were regularly preserved in brine or vinegar. Onions were an essential vegetable for the pot. The fruit was seasonal, mainly apples, pears, strawberries, and berries. Puddings were fruit tarts, rice pudding, cakes, often with spicing.[80] What was served at an ale, beer, cider house, or Inns, as centuries before and after, depended on the house's wealth or the Inn's clientele.[81] However, quality seems to

79. Celia Fiennes, *Through England on a side saddle in the Times of William and Mary*, London: Field and Tuer, The Leadenhall Press, 1888.
80. David Souden: *The Journals of the Hon. John Byng*, 1781–1792, edited 1991.
81. References in *Samuel Pepys Diaries*.

have been a mixed bag; plenty of novels have murmurings about burnt chops and poor-quality food.

The Little Parlour with its hearth, £6.05s: One table board and frame, two bedsteads, curtains & valances, one chair, two feather beds – *these were the mattresses*, two stools, two feather bolsters, one andiron, one fire shovel and tongues, three feather pillows, two flock bolsters, two pots, five blankets, one cushion.

It is helpful to remember that the many items in the Great Parlour were left to Edward Phipps or his son, aged 4, to be taken away after probate. It could be that those needed by his wife Thomasyn and son Francis had been moved into the little parlour at the time of the inventory.

The Brewhouse, £6.00: One furnace, one malt mill, items belonging to the cowhouse.

The Chamber over Brewhouse, £3.00: Twenty bushels of pulpo,[82] thirty wooden barrels, other items.

The West End Room, no hearth mentioned, £0.04s: One table board and frame, tressel and cloth.

The New Hall with Hearth, £4.00: One shovel, salt, two carpets, a small table, two chairs, twelve new stools, one square table board, a pair of andirons, four curtains, two pots with hearth tongs, fire shovel, two chairs.

---

82. Probably mash.

17th Century chair

The Pantry, £1.10s: One table board.

The New Cellar, £2.00: One salting tub, lamp fuel, three hogsheads, pots, bottles, other old things.

The new cellar was in the new building; its arch is visible today, externally, to the east of the passageway, at almost ground level.

The Old Cellar, £11.00: Two butts of wine - Roso, five hogsheads of wine or ale, two pipes *(port or wine)* and one empty hogshead, three bottles.

The old cellar would have been beneath the kitchen. The concept of a bar did not come about until the 19th Century. Instead, ale, beer or wine was served in pitchers or mugs and brought up straight from the barrels in the cellar. The typical English drinking mug ('the jack') was leather, waterproofed with pitch or beeswax. In the 18th Century, port was mentioned in diaries and other records.

In the 17th Century, water was not sufficiently safe; it was common for 6 or 7 quarts of ale, a weaker brew than today, to be drunk daily. Many inns brewed ale using just water, malt, yeast, and possibly the *herb mixture called gruit[83]. Broadway had several brew houses in homes, serving ale from the front door. It was a while before ale fell out of favour. Hops with their resins and oils, which stabilised and flavoured ale, had been grown from the start of the 15th Century, but Henry VI and Henry VIII had banned the use of the 'wicked and pernicious weed'. It was not until the fifth year of Edward VII, 1552, that privileges to hop growers were granted.[84] Eventually, people overcame their superstitions about the weed, got used to and liked their bitterness and appreciated the antibacterial properties of the resins within hops.*

The Half-Space, with no hearth, £0.10s: One table board and frame, two small drinks carriers and other.

The Great Parlour with hearth, £6.10s: One table board with frame, one press cupboard, one side cupboard, two chairs, two stools, three andirons, one fire shovel and tongs, three cushions, two carpets, one window curtain, one trundle bedstead, one high bedstead with curtains and pillows, one feather bed - *mattress*, two feather bolsters and two feather pillows, one flock bed and one flock bolster, two pairs of blankets.

83. Gruit is a herb mixture, it could vary by producer but may include common heather, ground ivy, horehound, mugwort, sweet gale, yarrow and juniper berries, ginger, caraway seed, aniseed, nutmeg, cinnamon, mint.
84. Knight Charles, *The Penny Magazine*, Charles Knight publisher, editor, and author 1832 issue

17ᵗʰ Century press cupboard

17ᵗʰ Century headbed with trundle bed curtains, bolster, and matress

Rooms on the ground floor opened into the street or yard. By a hearth, there might be a high-backed chair. The parlour served as dining, living, and sleeping space. Cupboards, chairs, curtains were prominent in this room, being associated with the master of the house.[85]

The New Room with hearth, £1.06.08d: A feather bed, one little table, curtains, one cupboard, one stool, andirons, fire shovel, pair of bellows, mats, other odd things.

In the same New Room, a linen store, £30.00: pillows, pillowcases, sheets, tablecloths, dusters, cupboard with napkins, towels, all differently described materials of the day, the reference to Holland associated with pillows, napkins, cloths may be to lace.

Even in a poor home, tablecloths were used as they had been for hundreds of years. Food was served on wooden trenchers or pewter plates, taken using a serving fork or spoon from a serving dish in the middle of the table. We were slow to take up the fork in England, so napkins were necessary.

---

85. The source of the term the 'chair-man' of the 'board'

1St Floor

The Chamber over the Kitchen, 6.15s: Five pots, one cupboard, three old bedsteads, three flock beds, three feather bolsters.

The Closet over the Kitchen, storage, £6.10s: Five silver cups, ten silver spoons, glass stored, copper pots.

The Gate House Chamber with hearth, £1.04s: One table board, a sub table, two chairs, two carpets, a window curtain, four stools, two cushions, andirons, fire shovel, tongs, and a pair of bolsters, one high bedstead and a trundle bed, mats, three blankets, two feather pillows and two feather bolsters.

The Great Chamber with hearth, estimate, £12.00: Four andirons, fire shovel, tongs, curtains, snuffers, a pair of bellows, two feather pillows, one bedstead, eight blankets, two carpets, three-room pots, cushions, a pair of curtains, three flock bolsters, flagons
Edward Phipps or his son, aged four, inherited all items in this room.

17th Century Andirons

17th Century Side table

The Green Chamber with hearth, £10.10s: One bedstead, a long table board and frame, one small table, one side cupboard, chairs, six stools, seven cushions, two carpets, a window cushion, three feather bolsters, three feather pillows, four blankets and more, a pair of andirons, fire shovel, hearth tongs

2nd Floor

The Hill Chamber with hearth, scant details, circa £8.00:
One bedstead, window curtain, two andirons, fire shovel, tongs
pair of bellows assume (some elements were unreadable) chair,
small table, stool, pillows, bolster, carpets, or mats

The Worcester Chamber with hearth, scant details, circa £8.00:
Two bedsteads, two andirons, fire shovel, tongs, bellows
- assume chair, small table, stool, pillows, carpets, or mats

The Angel Chamber with hearth,scant details, circa £8.00:
One bedstead, assume pillows, carpets and curtains, Pair of andirons,
fire shovel and tongs, iron dog. - assume chair, small table, stool,
pillows, carpets, or mats

White Chamber with hearth, estimated, £8.00: Joined bedstead,
pair of andirons, assume chair, small table, stool, pillows, carpets, or
mats

Rose Chamber, estimated, £1: One joined bedstead.

3rd Floor no hearths in the eaves

The Two-bed chamber, estimated, £1: One bedstead.
The Servants chamber estimated, £1: Two bedsteads.

Corn Chamber £32.15.06d
One tonne of coal, £1.6s.08d
Fourteen loads of firewood £4.10s
Timber in the street £2.10s
Two hundred boards in the stables £5.13.04d
Table boards in the stables £0.15s
Agricultural equipment £7.00
Mares and Geldings £24.00

Cows £21.00
Pigs £3.00
Wheat £20
Hay £8.00

An assessment on the value of the Inn for the life of his wife £30.00

Money in the house £10.00

The land behind the building, the backside, is also in the ownership of the freeholder but leased.

Chapter 9
Under the management of John Phipp's wife and son, 1673 - 1713

Following John's death in 1673, his wife, Thomasyn, managed the Inn with the help of her son Francis and their servants. Sadly, in 1677, she died, just four years after John. Just before her death, 10 October 1676, the Broadway register records the birth of Edward's daughter, Thomasyn (though misspelt Thomason), named in honour of her grandmother.

Unlike her late husband's will, Thomasyn's will, dated 10 December 1676, was a modest memorandum. The inventory of her goods and chattels, dated 17 November 1677, signed and countersigned respectively by her married daughter Ann Michell and one Alice Baker, merely identifies each room and a total value for the contents therein no other details. Detailing room contents may well have seemed unnecessary given her husband's full inventory, only four years earlier.

Whilst the room names remain almost the same in 1677 as in 1673, surprisingly, the estate's value of £173.11s.06d is 41% of the value of her husband's estate. As before, in 1673, around 40% of the wealth was linked to sources outside the Inn, i.e., geldings, pigs, corn, wheat and barley, wood, coal and timber. From the 1673 will, we know some lands had already passed to Edward and Francis. The impression given by the inventory is one of a somewhat reduced offer to the paying passengers; the Inn appears to be less refined, with a plainer interior.

With just the two family members and Thomasyn being in her mid - 60's when John died, more labour would have been required. That is unlikely to have been an added strain on the finances as servant labour was still relatively cheap, especially after taking off board and lodging. However, the increasing cost of maintaining and looking after the horses would have been a challenge.

The 1766 inventory, as mentioned, shows that the family no longer used the Great Chamber. It had become a communal bedchamber for those paying less and was called the five-bed chamber at her death. Passenger numbers were increasing, so there was a clientele more willing to share out of sheer necessity. Whilst the cost of accommodation would have been a factor for a traveller, more likely at this point in coaching development was the difficulty of finding a bed for the night.

In her will, Thomasyn left twenty shillings to the poor of the parish, twenty shillings apiece to her surviving children, and her wedding ring to her son Edward, probably because he had daughters and Francis was unmarried. No mention is made of her son William which suggests he had died between 1673 and 1676.

Thomasyn was laid to rest alongside her husband at the old church St Eadburgha's on the Snowshill Road, where their headstones should be found, had not the gravestones weathered, and the church records been destroyed in the dramatic floods of 2007.

John Phipps 99-year lease of the Angel, gardens and other lands was only legally applicable if he, his wife, or his son William were alive. With William fading from the records and no reference as to the future of the lease if all three had died, a new arrangement would seem to have been necessary. The term of lease remaining was around 80 years, depending on the actual date of its commencement.

John Phipps had left Edward and Francis financially independent of the Inn. Post-Thomasyn's death, with yet another generation to consider, Edward appears to have continued to remain financially independent of the Inn.

Regarding the remaining lease, Francis, who had been such a support to his widowed mother, appears to be the likely candidate. Indeed, the evidence points to him either taking up the remaining term of the lease or purchasing the freehold from Lord Coventry. He would not have been short of funds. He owned the tenements he had inherited from his father in 1673 and had received his £100 from Edward in 1676. He may not have purchased straight away in 1677, perhaps settling for the continuation of the lease arrangement.

We also know Francis had recovered unexpected funds in 1691 when an old debt harking back to 1687 was settled by the Broadway overseers[86] *"paid for expenses at the Angel when horses were pressed around the time of King James progress"*.[87] King James II abdicated in December 1688, which might explain why it took so long to claim the funds. Alternatively, when taking over from his mother, Francis could have discovered the sum had never been appropriated and set about rectifying the matter.

This debt suggests King James visited the Inn. Interestingly, this could explain a confusion two hundred years later when an owner of the property was under the impression King Charles had stayed at the Angel. Charles, I was dead before the Inn was built. Charles II visited Broadway, but there is no evidence Charles II ever visited the Angel. The Royal escape route from Worcester to Shoreham and France is well documented; it was not through Broadway.

Indeed, it appears that whether due to sound financial management and a good business sense, or the sum recouped from the debt related to James II, Francis had funds; and these funds could have been used to purchase the freehold.

---

86. Like a Parish Council. Overseers accounts Broadway papers, County Records.
87. The year before the he had abdicated, the 1687 King James' royal progress to Worcester. put Worcestershire again 'on the map.' Worcester was the first corporate town in which a mayor proclaimed Charles II at the Restoration.

Francis took over the running of the Inn after his mother died in 1677. Thomasyn's daughter Ann's son, Francis Michell, would later join his uncle to help run the Inn. He was the natural successor to the unmarried Francis after his father and mother had died, but in 1677 he was just a child.

Francis must have grown in confidence running the Inn. In 1700, thanks to additional records, we learn that Francis Phipps purchased another Inn, further down, on the other side of the street, the White Hart Inn,[88] from the dyers Thomas and Walter Parry. The purchase price was £159. One could surmise he thought he had no choice but to buy out the competition or was driven by a desire to dominate the industry and expand locally.

It is unlikely Francis would have funded the White Hart (Lygon Arms) purchase had he not already secured full ownership of the Angel. It is more likely his funds secured both establishments.

In 1713, coaching was still on the ascendancy, an expanding industry, additional routes were beginning to be mapped, and local carrier routes such as Cheltenham, Evesham, Gloucester, Worcester were emerging. Francis, an experienced Innholder, was now 58 years of age. Bearing in mind his father had died aged 66, this purchase may have fitted with his legacy planning. In addition, by 1700, his sister Ann's son, Francis Michell, who had by 1700 lived with him for some time, was just turning 26, therefore able to assume more responsibility.

As the old century ends and a new one begins, Francis Phipps, building on his legacy from his father, is now the proprietor of two of Broadways' most important and most complicated buildings and businesses.

---

88. Now The Lygon Arms.

Ten years later, around 1710, the Broadway register that recorded obligations to the local church and the maintenance of its walls confirms Francis Phipps as the owner of both the White Hart and the Angel and responsible for two sections of the wall. Whilst this is not 100% proof that Francis Phipps had bought the freehold of both the Angel, and the Lygon, in all probability, this seems to confirm the position regarding the two properties.

Occasionally entries in the Broadway register were signed by both the tenant and the subtenants, or freeholder and lessee in connection to their responsibility for a section of wall; this entry did not refer to any other freeholder or a subtenant.

Francis Phipps died, aged 71, in 1713, a wealthy man with an estate valued at £700. It was the end of an era for the first Innholder, John Phipps, and his immediate family. There is no mention of the Inn in Francis Phipps estate, which implies that it was passed to his nephew Francis Michell before his death.

Chapter 10
Under the ownership of Francis Phipps's nephew, Francis Michell, 1713-1749

On Francis Phipps death, in 1713, the estate passed to his nephew Francis Michell ' *who hath for many years lived with me in Broadway, my house …where John Griffiths, Clerk, now dwells, and that house or home stall called the White Hart, being a common Inn situated in Broadway, now inhabited by one John Cormell…., and all my yard lands and all my odd lands and commons in grass and pasture……all tenements and hereditaments whatsoever.*[89]

He also left £40 to the poor of Broadway that were not in receipt of any funds from the parish and £10 to his nieces, money to his sister, another nephew, and old servants.[90]

Mitchell had a good start, with such an inheritance and the promise of better coaching roads, following the first turnpike road in Worcestershire being improved in 1714. This improvement was a six-mile stretch from Droitwich to Worcester, the adoption by a turnpike company being prompted by the severe wear tear caused to those roads by the heavy salt wagons.

Initially, all seemed to have gone well, but as Michell reached middle age, he appears to have distanced himself from Broadway.

Evidence points to both inns, the Angel and the White Hart, being run by Innkeeper John Cormell and his stalwart wife, Ann, with supporting staff. Francis Michell, the freeholder, seems to have been happy for them to manage both for his and their benefit.

---

89. Curtis Garfield & Alison Ridley, *The Story of the Lygon Arms,* 1992.
90. Will of Francis Phipps, 15 March 1712, County Records.

Then, for reasons unknown, November 1732, despite the considerable inheritance provided by his uncle, Francis took out a £100 mortgage on the White Hart with one Sarah Taylor, thought to be related to the barrister William Taylor, the owner of the Middle Hill Estate. Unfortunately, we have no information on why he needed the £100.

John Cormell, possibly not long before he died, appears to have purchased the Angel. An 1882 abstract title between Isaac Averill in trust, under the will of Stephen Averill, to a messuage or dwelling house called Tudor House, to be sold, documents the location of Tudor House and says, " …….*and which said messuage and hereditaments were formerly the Estate of John Cormell deceased…….*"

In 1733, John Cormell, landlord[91] of the White Hart and owner of the Angel, died. Then in October 1734, Michell sold the White Hart, houses, and outbuildings to the late landlord's wife, Ann Cormell. This transaction was subject to the £100 mortgage of Francis Michell, now jointly held by Sarah (previously Taylor) and her husband, William Corbett, being extinguished.

After John died in 1734, Ann Cormell appears to have continued to manage the Angel and the White Hart (Lygon Arms) as the owner of the two properties. One wonders if the famous term 'Queen Ann', linked to a landlady in Broadway, applies to Ann Cormell. Sadly, there is nothing to confirm one way or another. Even with the support of her daughters and their husbands, it must have been some feat that she managed to run such two such large inns, even for seven years.

In 1739, just before she died, Ann borrowed firstly £50 from John Purser, who later would marry her daughter Mary, then slightly over

---

91. Up until 1733 records related to stage coaching seem to refer to innholders, inn's supplying post horses seem to refer to innkeepers, then landlords, then publican.

£200, a goodly sum, from a local man Isaac Averill senior.[92] She then put the White Hart (Lygon) into Trust for the two daughters, Mary and Sarah, who remained in Broadway.

The phrase 'formerly the Estate of John Cormell' referred to earlier in the text, and the information that Ann Cormell also put the White Hart (Lygon Arms) in Trust implies she may have been following John's lead; he had put his estate in Trust before he died.

We do not know why Ann needed the £50 or £200. It may be she was struggling after her husband John died. Ann's assets were now in Trust for her daughters, their children, and those children's children, and she died intestate.

Francis Michell died, aged 57, and was buried on 23 August 1749 at St Eadburgha's Church. There is no record of him having any interest in the Angel after 1733. Whether Francis Michell took his eye off the ball or whether competition and other factors affected the business is conjecture, but from the mid 18th Century, the Angel seems to have relinquished its position in terms of coaching supremacy.

In 1886, Andrew Carnegie (1835-1919), Scottish-American businessman, prominent philanthropist, and the founder of the Carnegie Steel Company, promoted a theory: *'three generations in America from shirt sleeves to shirt sleeves.'* [93] His harsh view was that the first generation builds the business, the second makes it a success, and the third wrecks it because the third generation does not have the same experience of having to work hard, struggle, and earn everything. He felt it was inevitable that the third generation would squander the wealth and lose it.

Given the increased competition in the village, such a judgement on Francis Michell could be deemed harsh. When his father ran the

_____

92. Father of Stephen Averill, Tudor House deeds 1881, uncle of Isaac Averill - younger.
93. This quote is habitually attributed to Andrew Carnegie, but it is disputed that he said it.

Angel, the village boasted a few common inns and outlying inns. However, by the early 18th Century, between 1720 and 1740, new inns had been built, or converted from farmhouses: The Woolpack[94] on one of the roads leaving Broadway, the Royal Exchange or George (1725), where the overseers (previously parish administrators) met, and The Bell or Old Bell [95] (1727), an alehouse or a home from which beer was sold, had sprung up on the road out of Broadway. The licence would later move to the centre of the village. There was also a plethora of houses selling ale, beer or cider.

After the death of Francis Michell and John and Ann Cormell and their lifetime's achievement, the freehold ownership of both the Angel and the White Hart is in Trust for future generations. The 1771 Inclosure Act award map recognised the ownership of the Angel JC, John Cormell. However, as John has been dead for thirty-eight years, we can only surmise the reference was to the Trust in his, not his wife's name, as he was the owner originally.

By mid 18th Century, the village continued to be hostage to the stage coaching industry; new inns, ale, beer sellers, and cider houses were all on the bandwagon. As well as the competition, costs are rising, making a profit is getting harder. At the end of the 18th Century, the introduction of the mail coach would push the boundaries even more. Some will significantly benefit from this change; others will not. The one aspect of the mail coaches to come will be their single-mindedness. They will be driven by speed, the need to deliver on time, the need for providers, the coaching companies, and the inns

---

94. The site of Tower View House demolished 1911, due to its location on the route from Broadway, colloquially known as Ketch 'em at the end.
95. The property became a homestead in the 19th Century and was merged into an extension of a neighbouring property, Court Farm, in the early 20th Century.
.

they contract with to be reliable. Passengers will become a secondary consideration.

Chapter 11

Turnpikes, Mail Coaches, improved Road Design, 1750-1830

At the end of the 17th Century, Parliament had made it understood that it would take responsibility for repairing and maintaining roads away from local authorities to improve them. It then started to pass a series of Turnpike Acts authorising not-for-profit trusts to levy tolls on those using their routes and to use that income to repair and improve specific roads. When necessary, the turnpike trusts could use their powers to purchase property to widen or divert existing roads.

These Trusts were an essential part of English life from 1690 to 1840. By the end of this period, 20,000 miles of road had been turnpiked nationally; many are the roads we travel today.

Nationally between 1751-72, "turnpike mania" resulted in the trusts being responsible for more than 11,500 miles of road; over half of the existing roads then would eventually become turnpike roads in England.

Milestones usually evidenced a turnpike road. In the upper part of Broadway's High Street, the milestone erected against the wall to the right of the door to Milestone House has hewn on its face the distance to London, 90 miles. This was a practical confirmation of mapmaker Daniel Patterson's [96] measurement (94 miles). The plaque below reminds us that during the second world war, all milestones in England were deliberately defaced; the distances on signs were cut

---

96. Daniel Paterson (1739–1825), a significant British army officer and cartographer.

or rubbed off, totally obliterated, in order not to aid the enemy should there have been an invasion. The signage was re-carved in 1953.

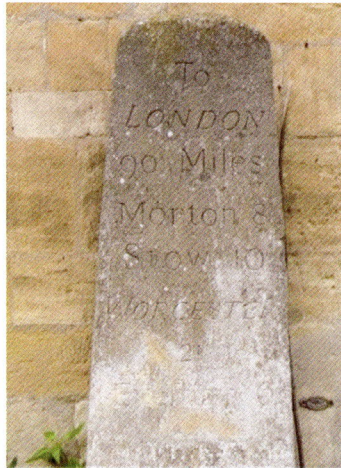

Milestone next to Milestone House, in the upper part of the High Street

However, by the mid 19th Century, the gains would decline, and coaching would leave the turnpike companies struggling financially.

Being in the provinces, Worcestershire did not fare as well as other counties. Whilst the first turnpike in England was built in 1663, a ploy to encourage those investing in coaching houses, the first turnpike in Worcestershire was early 18th Century, 1728; the Evesham Turnpike Trust took responsibility for the Fish Hill to Worcester Road, now known as the A44.

It would not be until 1824 that the Mickleton and Broadway and Chipping Campden Trust was formed to improve the Leamington Road from Broadway to Mickleton.

Despite the steady expansion of coaching enterprises, the turnpikes were slow to make a difference. The necessary road improvements just did not materialise in a way that kept pace with the need.

However, thanks to the turnpike funding innovators such as John Loudon MacAdam[97] (1756-1836) and Thomas Telford [98] (1757-1834), the Regency period (1811-1820) saw their ideas turn into changes on the ground, significantly improving journeys and journey times.

Finally, by 1805 there were the longed-for metalled roads.

Whilst journeys were becoming increasingly straightforward; they were still risky in many other ways. 24 May 1759, Berrows, Worcester Journal, reported that

> *The stage wagon belonging to Mr Tanner of Worcester, while on its way back from London, caught fire in the vicinity of Broadway. It was thought that the fire had been caused by a bottle of nitric acid bursting. Much of the valuable load, which included a quantity of fine silks, was either destroyed or severely damaged. According to the newspaper the unfortunate Mr Tanner had only recently sustained a, "considerable loss", when his wagon overturned whilst crossing the River Avon. They predicted that he would be saved from ruin because the owners of the goods he was carrying would, "through compassionate concern", bear part of the loss. [99]*

Slow speeds remained an issue for both the passengers and the mail.

Innovation came in the form of the renowned Bristol and Bath theatre impresario, John Palmer (1742-1818). He used coaches to

---

97. McAdam, surveyor to the Bristol Turnpike Trust in 1816, decided to remake the roads under his care with crushed stone bound with gravel on a firm base of large stones. This, the greatest advance in road construction since Roman times, became known as "macadamisation ".
98. Telford was responsible for rebuilding sections of the London to Holyhead Road. He introduced the idea of making the road slightly convex, ensuring rainwater rapidly drained off the road rather than penetrate and damage the road's foundations.
99. 24 May 1759, Berrows, Worcester Journal.

move his actors around the country to ensure all the actors were in the same place at the same time.

Palmer revolutionised the postal service by proposing the Royal Mail replace postboys on horseback with armed men on fast, dedicated, lightweight coaches. He complained about the time it took a letter from Bath to reach London by the 8-horse carts, known as *'slow coaches'*, which ran at about two miles per hour ' *the Mail is generally entrusted to some idle boy without character, mounted on a worn-out hack who so far from being able to defend himself or escape from a robber is more likely to be in league with him...*' [100]

In 1782, he suggested that the Post Office in London adopt his proposal. Unsurprisingly he met resistance from officials who believed that the existing system could not be improved. Eventually, the Chancellor of the Exchequer, William Pitt, allowed him to carry out an experimental run between Bristol and London. Palmer funded the trial run on the Bristol-to-London route in 1784.[101] The coach completed the 116 miles in a record sixteen hours rather than the usual thirty-eight and continued to do so for the whole week of the trial. The experiment's success persuaded Parliament that mail coaches could transport letters and parcels faster, safer, and more efficiently than riders.

Very soon afterwards, the mail coaches were running through England. The first record of a mail coach stopping in Broadway at the Bell is 1788. Mail coaches ran to new tight and regular timetables at a respectable average speed of 10 miles per hour. Horses were

---

100 Attributed to John Palmer in J. Wilson Hyde, *One Hundred Years by Post*, Sampson Low, Marston & Co, LIM
101. *The Mail Coach Service,* The British Postal Museum & Archive.

changed very speedily; one minute[102] was allowed to take out the old horses and harness up a fresh team.

> *It was a pretty sight to see the changing of the horses, there stood the fresh team, two on the offside, two on the near side, and the coach was drawn up with the utmost exactitude between them. Four ostlers jumped to the splinter bars and loose the traces; the reigns have already been thrown down. The driver retains his seat, and within the minute (more than once within fifty seconds by the watch), the coach begins its onward journey.'* [103]

Mail coaches did take paying passengers, but the mail was of primary importance. If there were an accident or bad weather, the passengers would be left at the side of the road while the mail was carried on foot or horseback to the nearest town.

By 1797, there were forty-two coach routes throughout the country, linking most major cities and carrying both stage and mail coaches.

---

102. To put this in perspective, though not quite as fast, it would have seemed, the equivalent to the spectacle of a wheel change on a Formula I Grand Prix car.
103. Thomas Trollope, brother of Anthony, Travel Writer.

The London Mail Coach leaving Worcester at the end of the 18th Century

The crested mail coaches, often red, now sped across the country with their guards, ex-soldiers, standing on the mailboxes, heavily armed with blunderbusses and the like.

Broadway's wealth had moved away from fleece and agriculture, had again grown as stage coach travel had taken off through the latter half of the 17th Century and the 18th Century.

Across England, some innkeepers were making a good living from accommodation and livery. In major towns, inns could have had some 50 or 60 horses available in their yards. Profitability, as always, depended on adaptability.

Speed and the strict timetable were taking over from comfort, accommodation, selling beds or providing meals. Coaching was increasingly risky, resulting in additional costs to address the risks. Coach design had improved to include more safety features, but they came with a heavy price tag. It could take two years to recover the capital outlay. The working life of a coach horse added up to 3 -4 years at best. Overall, there were slimmer margins. And the Angel did not fare well in the next period.

From the early 19th Century, inns margins decreased. The first stage coaches ran during the day and stopped at night, a routine known as inning, but by the 19th Century, speed was of the essence; mail coaches ran both day and night. As a result, costs and risks increased, and the margins were lower. The days of leisurely meals, sleeping over, and the profits they brought were slipping away.

Chapter 12
The Angel Inn and the Bell Inn
1771 - 1840

From the mid 18th Century, there was considerable churn in the licencing and accommodation arrangements in Broadway.

It was not unusual for licences and names to move; in 1791, the Swan's licence was transferred from Russell House, Lower Green, across the road, to two cottages, on the Green now the much extended (new) Swan Inn. Later, the Kettle opposite the Angel Inn was renamed the New Inn when the New Inn's licence moved from the old Midland Bank site.[104]

Larger inns were now common, new inns were springing up, and inns besides major highways were growing in grandeur. What is known, so far, of inns in Broadway and their development over the years forms an appendix to this book, a complex and separate area of ongoing research.

This book now focuses on other inns that appear to have impacted the fortunes of the Angel, starting with the Bell Inn. The story of the Bell has a level of complexity related to the movement of its licence. It is possible that when the Bell could not accommodate the Licence as it was a ladies Seminary, it moved across the way to the Angel or Crown.

The licence of the Old Bell Inn is said to have moved from an older Inn, part of which dated back to the 14th Century, located on the

---

104. Previously The Midlands Bank then HSBC, now a private apartment and commercial building.

road out of Broadway, [105] called either The Bell or Old Bell. However, when post-1771, the road up Broadway Hill, out of Broadway, was altered, the new route passed very close to a summer house on either the Farncombe or the Coventry's estate.[106] This summer house was reconfigured to become the Fish Inn, resulting in The Bell or Old Bell Inn losing its trade due to the route change and reverting to a Farmhouse.[107] [108]

A very early photograph of the Fish Inn building 18th Century – there appears to be no extension behind the building, just a wall.

105. A list 1924, J Morris.
106. Evidence supports both theories.
107. Bell House Farm was subsequently absorbed, by architect A N Prentice, into Court Farm in the early 20th Century.
108. A list 1924, J Morris.

The new Bell Inn,[109] the recipient of the transferred licence, was situated in the centre of the village, the property now known as Picton House.

Picton House

This fine early 18th Century, two-story house, of limestone ashlar[110], with a stone slate roof, may have been built as a farm or manor house. No records have yet been found to corroborate its build date. The family name associated with the house is Stretch. Its fine pair of gates are said[111] to have originally graced the entrance to Broadway's 'Great Farme',[112] opposite St Eadburgha's church,

109. Picton House, 42 High Street, adjacent to Bell Yard, Bell Cottage.
110. Fine cut limestone.
111. Dr Colin Houghton: Broadway Pictorial, page 13.
112. The 'Greate Farme', later known as Broadway Court, is thought to have started life as a small monastic building and lands, leased to Anthony Daston of Dumbleton in the 16th

demolished around 1773 by George Savage to build a property known as Middle Hill.

It has also been suggested, though not evidenced, that the fine ashlar stone used in the Bell's construction was part of the remaining stone from the 'Greate Farme.' If true, this could support the theory that the building of property known as the Bell, now Picton House, including the addition of the gates, took place after 1733.

Before the Bell's licence was associated with this property, it was known to be a Tory house, called either The George or The King's Head.

Between 1770 –1771, it was the base for a commissioner's inquiry into the dividing and inclosing the open and common fields and common lands within the Manor of Broadway in preparation for a local Inclosure Act.[113] For the inquiry, Broadway's fields and lands were surveyed and delineated [114] by Thomas Webb and Francis Webb, thought to be father and son, with a Stanway connection. Their determination required a great deal of local engagement, as would any public inquiry today. Eventually, the common land of Up

---

Century, by the Abbot of Pershore, shortly before the dissolution of the monasteries. In 1539 the land fell to the Crown but was subsequently purchased from Queen Mary, by a court favourite, William Babington, in July 1558. (Harleian Manuscripts in the British Museum). 1573/4 William Babington's grandson sold the property and lands to Daston's widow, Ann, who as a result became Broadway's largest landowner (2960 acres). All that remains of the property today is the gate house, said to have been to the stables, a decayed building in 1898 which was remodelled by Guy Dawber at the end of the 19th Century to become Court House now known as Broadway Court.

113. A series of Acts (1760 - 1870) that empowered enclosure of open fields and common land in England. The Inclosure Acts use an old or formal spelling of the word. It is now more usually spelt "enclosure".

114. The Tithe Survey represented the first systematic mapping survey that covered most of England and Wales. Maps were not a required part of the Inclosure process until 1801 so not all Inclosure Acts have maps. Where there is a 19th Century Inclosure Act map for a Parish, there is usually not a Tithe map. This is the case for much of the south-east of Worcestershire. There is also a caveat that Inclosure Act maps are generally the proposed layout of the fields and may not be what happened when the land was finally enclosed.

End[115] was enclosed, and the great and small tithes of Broadway Manor, the property of the lay impropriators[116] and vicar, were commuted. The dissolution of the monasteries in 1539 had led to the seizing of land, by lay people or a lay person, from the church, so the commissioners took the opportunity to regulate ownership.

The changes arising from the Act significantly influenced the landscape [117] we see around us today. A handy product of the Inquiry that aids historians today are the local Manor of Broadway's Awards maps.

Confirmation that the property became the Bell Inn after the commissioners left comes from a regional newspaper dated 4 December 1779. [118] The newspaper announced a forthcoming auction of a freehold property in Broadway to be held at the Bell Inn. It also tells us the name of the innkeeper. The Bell was the house of Richard Davis. We learn more of Richard's business from an advertisement in the same newspaper,[119] 10 May 1788.

---

115. Upper End is the medieval name for the land from the Green to St Eadburgha's Church and up to Seven Sisters.

116. A term from English ecclesiastical law, relates to the destination of the income from tithes. When the monastic properties passed into lay hands at the Reformation, many takings of land were converted into tithes going to lay people.

117. The main sources of information for these changes are maps documenting the details of Inclosure in the late 18th and early 19th centuries and the mid 19th century assessment of holdings during the survey of the Tithe Commissioners.

118. Oxford Journal, 4 December 1779. TO be SOLD by AUCTION, By JOSEPH PRATT, On Friday the 17th Day of December Instant, at the House of Richard Davis, commonly called or known by the Name or Sign of the Bell Inn, situated and being at Broadway, the County of Worcester, A Freehold Stone-built or Tenement ....

119. Oxford Journal 10 May 1788 BELL INN, BROADWAY, Worcestershire. RICHARD DAVIS I") BEGS Leave to return his most humble and sincere thanks to the Nobility, Gentry, and the Public at large, for the many favours with which they have honoured him during his Residence in the above Inn; and at the same time begs leave to inform them, that the said Inn is fitted up for the Reception Company, in neat Stile whom he will furnish with the first and best accommodations, and therefore hopes may look forward for their future Patronage. The said Richard Davis, at the request of Thomas Kirk of Chapel-House, acquaints the Public, that the said T. Kirby, for the more effectual accommodation of his Friends, and

STAGECOACHES from Worcester to London. The Two-day Coach sets out from the Bell, in Broad-Street, Worcester, every Monday, Wednesday, and Friday Morning; stops at the Bell' Inn. Broadway, for Passengers to drink Tea, and change Horses, at Ten o'Clock. Returns from London the said Inn to Dinner, every Tuesday, Thursday, and Saturday, at One o Clock. The OLD FLY[120] sets out from the Coach-Office, Worcester, every Day the Week, except Thursday {stops at the said Inn for Passengers to drink Tea and change Horses at Five o Clock in the Afternoon; returns every Day in the Week, except Friday, Five o Clock in the Morning. Five ?? in the Morning. The MAIL COACH sets out from "the Hop- Pole every Evening, stops at the said Inn at Six o'Clock, and returns every Morning at Nine; stops to change Horses at the above Inn, both in going and returning. Parcels to go the above Conveyance will be taken due Care of.

The Inn was sold just before Richard Davis's death, 20 May 1790; therefore, it is reasonable to presume he was in poor health at the time of the sale.

Furthermore, the Oxford Journal, 23 April 1790, records that one Thomas Bolton, late waiter from the King's Head, Gloucester,

---

to tender travelling on the road more expeditious the Chaise Line, intends for the future, (with their permission) to drive to the Inn ; and that the said R. Davis will exert his utmost endeavours to give them ample satisfaction, as good horses and careful drivers will be kept to go any part of the Kingdom.

120. A renowned mail coach.

purchased the Bell [121]and that the Aurora and the mail coach[122] both stopped at this Inn.

What then happened to the Bell between Thomas Bolton's purchase in 1790 and the inn's sale, thirty years later, in 1820, is intriguing. In March 1809, auction particulars[123] described the property as the former Bell, a mansion, which had become an Academy,[124] run by Mrs Smith, a tenant at will.[125] Her husband, the former innkeeper of the Bell, was being forced to sell as he had been declared bankrupt.

Somehow the tenacious lady acquired ownership in 1809.

5 August 1809, Mrs Smith placed an advertisement[126] advising the parents and guardians of the young ladies in her care that *'her partnership with a Miss Kempson is, by mutual agreement,*

---

121. Oxford Journal, THOMAS BOLTON, late Waiter from the Kings Head, Gloucester, having purchased and entered upon the above Inn, most respectively informs the Nobility, Gentry, and the Public, that the Inn is elegantly and commodiously fitted for their Reception ; and assures as well the Friends of his Predecessor, as his own Friends, and the Public, that is determined to exert his utmost endeavours to furnish them with good Accommodations, the best Wines, and every other Article, on the most reasonable Terms humbly hoping, his Assiduity, to merit their Protection and Support. Good Stall Stabling; and neat Post Chaises the Notice. N, R. The Aurora, or Morning Coach, Breakfast at the above Inn, every Morning Seven o'clock; and or the Return drinks tea every Evening at Six, Sundays excepted. Likewise, the Mail Coach (stops at the above Inn, both going to London and coming back. The greatest Care will be taken of Parcels, and forwarded, directed, with Expedition.
122. The Royal Mail from London or Worcester.
123. SOLD by AUCTION, By T. JARRETT, at the White Hart Inn, Broadway, in the county of Worcester, on Wednesday the 22nd day of March Inst. Between the hours of three and four of the clock in the afternoon ; LOT I.—All that capital stone built MANSION, situate in the centre of Broadway aforesaid, with the Garden and Appurtenances thereunto belonging, formerly known the name of the Bell Inn, but now and for several years past used an Academy, in the occupation of Mrs. Smith, tenant at will. LOT 11.— Two good Stables, with spacious Granaries over the same, near to lot 1; one thereof the possession Mrs Smith, and the other in hand.
124. In this context Academy is a girl's school, seminary teaching social etiquette and the three r's
125. A tenancy or license at will is a short, flexible tenancy or license and in most respects is more like a licence than a tenancy. A tenancy-at-will is from the outset intended to be short and can be terminated at any time by either party.
126. Worcester Journal 10 August 1809.

dissolved.' She advises she has been in Broadway for 16 years, since 1793, and that she is taking over the debts of the old firm.

Nine years later, on 19 October 1820, different auction particulars, again describe the property as the former Bell, built in a most substantial manner, that had been run as a Ladies Seminary,[127] for 30 years (1790-1820), by the same Mrs Smith. The 30 years claim is at odds with her previous announcement that she came to Broadway in 1793.

It can be concluded that a Thomas Bolton, waiter, who purchased the inn in 1790, was not a successful innkeeper, nor was his successor Mr Smith. Still, Mrs Smith had kept the wolf from the door by running an Academy for around 16 years and a Seminary for a further ten years until 1820. Thus, for a good part of 27 years, 1793-1820, the Bell's licence could well have been transferred to another property.

In the next chapter, we consider whether the Bell's licence transferred across the street, now the High Street, to the Angel, the Crown next door to the Angel or both, and if so, for how long?

---

127. TO BE SOLD BY AUCTION, BY MR. W. HOBBS,' At the While Hart Inn, Broadway, Worcestershire, Thursday, the 19th day of October, 1820, at three o'clock; A Capital FREEHOLD DWELLING-HOUSE, built in most substantial manner, and in good repair, with very superior Garden, planted with the finest productive fruit trees, inclosed by very lofty wall, situate in the centre of the healthy town of Broadway an agreeable distance from the great turnpike road to London and Worcester now in the occupation of Mrs Smith the Proprietor, who has established and carried it on as a Ladies' Seminary for near thirty years with the greatest success, for which it is admirably calculated, possessing the advantages of spacious Premises and good situation ; together with the good-will the Establishment, which is now in high repute, and promises every success to any one capable of undertaking the management it. May viewed Mondays, Wednesdays, and Saturdays, when particulars may had of Mrs. Smith, on the Premises; of Henry Sykes, Esq. Gloucester; of Mr. Wall, and of Mr. Hobbs, Auctioneer, Worcester.

To finish our story of the Bell, in 1820, it was purchased by the Ashwins[128] , a young couple in their mid-twenties, to run as an inn and a school. They were an enterprising couple.

On Tuesday, 1 November 1842, the Bell, Broadway played host to The Independent Order of Odd Fellows, Manchester Unity, Loyal Saxon Lodge, 3352. The officers of the Cheltenham district opened the new Lodge base at the house of William Ashwin, a member of the lodge. Twelve tradesmen were initiated into the mysteries of Odd Fellowship,

> *And though 'the minds of several of them had been operated upon the absurd rumours regarding odd-fellows and their mysteries which caused them little trepidation, few minutes passed in the company of the brethren soon dissipated any feeling of fear, and anxiety soon gave way to happiness'. At five o'clock a capital dinner was served up by the worthy host, 'and nearly forty gentlemen and brothers from Cheltenham, Evesham, and other parts partook, under the able presidency of Prov. O.M. Parker, who was well supported by P.V. Smith, of Evesham. The usual loyal toasts being given, several capital songs and speeches from the chairman, Prov. D.G.M. Shenton, Past. Prov. G.M. Draper, and other brothers, neat band of music kept alive the interval till about nine o'clock, and the evening was finished merrily yet wisely, by dance, in which the wives and sweethearts of the members joined, and thus shared with their best protectors the enjoyment of the day.[129]*

As to the coaching at the Bell and Broadway, we know the following:

---

128. Thought to be related to the Ashwins of Willersey.
129. Gloucestershire Chronicle - Saturday 05 November 1842.

In 1788 the two-day coach, and Old Fly ran through Broadway and stopped at the Bell, as did the Mail Coach.

In 1790, Thomas Bolton told us the Aurora runs from the Bell through his advertisement.

In 1825[130] the Royal Mail, Telegraph, and Aurora passed through Broadway and had renewed relationships with the Bell.

In 1828[131] the Royal Mail ran daily from Worcester, as did the Sovereign. They were both accommodated at the Lygon Arms. The focus of these coaches would have been speed and the timetable, not accommodation for passengers. The Lygon Arms was ideal. It had many good stables. The Aurora, the Old Fly and the Telegraph went through Broadway, but we do not know from which inn they ran.

Joseph Clew of Ludlow ran carriers on a Wednesday, Jolly every Wednesday, Saturday and Sunday, and J and C Ward from Evesham on a Tuesday and a Saturday.

In 1835 references[132] are to The Royal Mail, The Telegraph, and the Sovereign but not the Old Fly or the Aurora.

By 1840 only six inns, now called taverns, are recorded in Broadway: The Sovereign calls at the Bell, the Mail Coach at the Lygon Arms, and a new coach, the Monarch, is added. There is no mention of the Old Fly, Aurora, or the Telegraph.

The entry in Bentley's Trade Directory 1840 refers:
TAVERNS
Bell, - Ashwin

---

130. Pigot's 1825 Directory.
131. Pigot's 1828 Directory.
132. Pigott's 1835 Directory.

Boot - John Castle
Crown and Trumpet, T. Clark
Lygon's Arms, Charles Drury, (Commercial and Posting)
Swan, Joseph Hawkes
White Horse, Israel Charlwood
COACHES - Broadway 1840

To LONDON:

Sovereign calls at the Lygon's Arms every morning (Sunday, excepted) at half-past 10. fare same as mail. The Royal Mail from Worcester calls at the Lygon's Arms every evening at 8: fare 30s. and 16s.
The Monarch calls at the Bell every evening (Sundays excepted) at half-past 8.

To WORCESTER:

The Royal Mail from London calls at the Lygon's Arms every morning a quarter past 6: fare 10s. and 5s. The Sovereign at quarter past four afternoons.
The Monarch calls at the Bell every morning at half-past 6.
They go through Evesham and Pershore

There are still many questions still to be answered. For example, when did the stage coach or stage coaches stop calling at the Angel? What caused them to cease using the Angel? Between 1790 and 1820, where did the Aurora stop?

In the next chapter, we explore the interrelationship between the Angel, Bell and Crown and Crown.

Chapter 13
The Angel Inn, The Bell and Crown, The Crown Inn, 1771 - 1855

In the latter part of the 18th Century and early 19th Century, Broadway saw an expansion in the number of ale, beer, and cider houses and new inns along Broadway Street.[133] As the new century dawned, the stories of the Angel, the Bell and Crown, the Crown, and the Bell further down Broadway Street seem to be intertwined.

It is clear for a good period between 1793 and 1820, the Bell, a known Inn on the main street, was not trading; it was an academy or seminary. Mrs Smith, at one time, through her advertisements and auctions, says for 26 years and another time says 30 years.

The Angel 1771- 1834

After John and Ann Cormell died in 1733 and 1740, respectively, the Angel and the White Hart (Lygon Arms) were in a Trust. This arrangement benefited the two of her daughters who chose to remain in Broadway and their families.

The Award map shows the site of the Angel belonged to JC, John Cormell or his Trust. It also identifies John Cormell owns thirty-two acres, three rods and three perches, northwest of the town, north of

---

the turnpike[134] to Worcester.[135] So again, up to 1771, we form an impression that innkeeping was a reasonably prosperous business.

Concerning the White Hart, the Cormell daughter's (and their husband's) dealings are described as a series of complex financial transactions, a long and disjointed series of borrowings. [136] There is no reason to think their dealings regarding the Angel were dissimilar. They appear to have been hands-off innkeeper's and used their assets as collateral whenever they required funds.

After the Cormell's, the deeds tell us that Mary Davis[137] became the last known innkeeper at the Angel. Mary Davis, born Wallen, had married Richard Davis,[138] the Innkeeper of the Bell, in 1758. After his death, on 20 May 1790, the Bell was sold on 17 December 1790. Mary then appears to have moved across the road to become the innkeeper at the Angel.

---

134. A network of well-maintained roads was one of the major achievements of 18th Century England. These highways facilitated the rapid and efficient transportation of goods and passengers throughout the Kingdom, reducing costs and forming an integrated, free market.

135 The turnpike, thought locally to have been run by the Evesham to Stow Trust, established in 1727, was the gate that blocked the road until a toll was paid.

136. Curtis Garfield & Alison Ridley, *Story of the Lygon Arms*, 1992, page 100.

137. The 1881 extract of deeds of Tudor House, previously the Angel Inn.

138. The Oxford Journal December 4, 1779, refers to a Bell Inn where an auction of another property is to take place: TO be SOLD by AUCTION, By JOSEPH PRATT, On Friday the 17th Day of December Instant, at the House of Richard Davis, commonly called or known by the Name or Sign of the Bell Inn, situated and being at Broadway, the County of Worcester, —A Freehold Stone-built or Tenement, with the Garden, Orchard, Barn, and Stables to the same belonging and adjoining; also three closes or Inclosure of good Pasture Ground to the Premises belonging, (situated and being in Broadway aforesaid. The buildings in general are in good Repair, and the Orchard is planted with good Fruit Trees, and the other Inclosures are well timbered and watered. The Tenant, William Dobbins, will shew the Premises; and farther Particulars may had applying Mr. John Phillips, or Mr. Pratt, the Auctioneer, in Evesham, in the County of Worcester aforesaid.

After Mary, the inn was repurposed. John Stanley purchased it sometime before 1834.[139] Stanley, a timber merchant of Broadway, had then leased the property and its lands to William Cotterill, a local farmer.[140] Deeds also record Stanley renewed his lease with Cotterill for fourteen years; it is fair to assume the first lease was also for fourteen years.

This would put Stanley's purchase date around 1820, which fits a record confirming the Aurora returned to its relationship with the Bell, not the Angel, in 1825. By circa 1820, Angel's building and land had been decoupled. The house and garden and its garden could be leased or sold.

The Bell and Crown 1797-1855

Records of a Bell and Crown can be found between 1797 – 1814 and its sale in 1855. It is referred to in numerous auction catalogues and as a meeting place for settling estate matters such as:

- 5 September 1797, the auction of Collin Farm, a house, and meadows let to a Mr Averill (*Snr*) and lands near the Pools was held at the Bell and Crown.[141]
- 1799 catalogues for livestock sales could be picked up at the Bell and Crown.
- 18 November 1809,[142] The Bell and Crown was the location for particulars of a large sale of stock from Kites Nest Farm.
- 23 November 1809, The Bell and Crown[143] is one of the locations holding catalogues concerning a cow stock auction.

---

139. Described in the 1881 extract of deeds relating to Tudor House, previously the Angle Inn.
140. 1834 the lease is a repeat lease of an earlier arrangement.
141. The Oxford Journal 19th August 1797 and 26th August 1797.
142. Worcester Journal.
143. Ibid.

- 1 March 1810, The Bell and Crown[144] is a location for picking up catalogues concerning a sale of ash and underwood.
- 23, 24, 25, September 1812, The Bell and Crown was the location of a three-day auction, including the stock of a local cabinet maker and upholsterer.
- 26 November 1812, [145] The Bell and Crown is the location for the auction of the Malt House and property of Sir T. E. Winnington.
- 17 September 1812,[146] a sale of modern household furniture, at auction J. Richardson, on Wednesday, Thursday, Friday, 23, 24, 25 September, in the commodious rooms at the Bell and Crown, Broadway, Worcestershire. Interestingly, in some of the auction particulars, the descriptions reveal how taste, travel, and trade had changed; the contents of a house in the 18th Century had an added degree of sophistication compared with those noted in Phipps 17th Century inventory.

An assemblage useful, elegant, and modern FURNITURE, and other effect, part of the Stock of a Cabinet-Maker and Upholsterer, consigned and removed for convenience of sale: Comprising sixteen plain and drapery four-post and tent with bedsteads and furniture, fitted up with straw and wool mattresses, superfine seasoned goose other feather beds, bolsters and pillows, blankets and counterpanes, floor and bedside carpets, pier and dressing glasses, mahogany dressing tables, basin stands and chests with drawers, set mahogany Cumberland dining tables, ditto on pillars and claws, Pembroke, card, sofa, pillar and night ditto, two sets drawing room chairs, with cushions and Grecian scroll couches to correspond,

144. Ibid.
145. Ibid.
146. Ibid

mahogany chairs and sofas, three handsome side-boards, mirrors, japanned tea trays and caddies, with a great variety useful chamber and other articles.

- 5 April 1814, a bankruptcy hearing was held at the Bell and Crown.[147]

The Crown 1771 - 1826

A much smaller building than the Angel, this two-story building, with an attic floor, was built to a quality standard; like its neighbour, it is limestone ashlar with a stone slate roof. Though listed as being built in 1774, it appears on the 1771 Award map to the east of the Angel, attributed to Lord Coventry, most likely that of the Right Honourable George William 6th Earl of Coventry [148] (1722– 1809).

The Crown, now Eadburgha House, the Chimneys are the Angel's

---

147. Northampton Mercury 19 March 1814.
148. Ten years earlier, in 1761, Sir George had inherited his title, the Croome Estate near Pershore and had been heavily involved in organising a house on the Spring Hill Estate, for his brother the 5th Earl.

The messuage, fully described in deeds,[149] offers a long boundary to the Angel. No rear entrance to the property is visible on the map, but it is known[150] to have once provided stabling for the Coventry's horses.[151]

The 1881 Abstract of Title, for the sale of Tudor House, is precise as to Tudor House's location and says *"....having the Street or Highway leading through Broadway to London on the North, a close then or late called Broad Close on the South and West and a messuage formerly known as the Crown Inn on the east side thereof...."* Still in situ, on the front of the building, is a dated keystone above its Haulway which suggests the entrance to its yard was enlarged in 1774, possibly to take commercial coaches, suggesting it became an inn at this date.

Keystone -The Crown Inn

149. Ibid.
150. now Eadburgha House.
151. Possibly to pull his private coach up Fish Hill.

Curiously, almost no records of the Crown have come to light between 1774 -1826, a newspaper announcement[152] of a sale supports the Crown ceasing to be an inn in 1826, notably the details of the quantities of ale, cider, and wines, to be sold.

Neat and modern Household Furniture, WINES, LIQUORS, ALE, CIDER, BREWING REQUISITES, &c. To be SOLD by AUCTION, by G. HALFORD,[153] on Tuesday, Wednesday, and Thursday next, the 11th, 12th, and 13th of April, 1826, on the premises of Mr. Edward Halford, at the Crown Inn, Broadway, Worcestershire, who is leaving that part of the country; comprising 15 mahogany four-post, tent, and other bedsteads, clothed in neat dimity, chintz, and cotton furniture's, 15 prime seasoned feather and flock beds[154], several pairs of large Whitney blankets, counterpanes, quilts, and bedding; handsome sets of mahogany and oak dining, card, Pembroke, pillar and claw, dressing, and other chairs, neat mahogany sitting room, chamber, parlour, and kitchen chairs, pier and swing glasses, chests of drawers, wash-hand stands and tables, night conveniences, wool and straw mattresses, floor, bedside, and stair carpets, eight-day clocks, china and glass dinner services, fenders and fire-irons, pots, kettles, &c ; 130-gallon and smaller copper furnaces, mash, rearing, and 'washing tubs, coolers, 8 very capital iron-bound 200-gallon, and smaller casks, tubs, pails, &c.; several dozens of old Port and Sherry Wines, Brandy, Rum, and Gin, about 1,000 gallons of good Ale, 130 gallons of prime Cider, with numerous other effects, which are expressed in Catalogues, to be had at the place of sale; and Inns in the neighbourhood. Sale to commence at Eleven o'clock precisely, and, as the proprietor is leaving the country, there will be no reserve.

---

152. Oxford Journal – Saturday 1 April and Saturday 8 April 1826.
153. G Halford was either Edward's father or his half brother.
154 Probably mattresses.

The Auction is on the premises at the Crown Inn.

The Crown is not a large building, it only has two floors, and one is in the attic. Its layout may have been very different in 1774, but it would seem only to accommodate, especially given it has few chimneys, five or six bedrooms. Therefore, it is puzzling to see how fifteen mahogany four-post were housed. In addition, the cellar contents suggest a larger premise.

Could the other rooms have been in the Angel? Did the Crown join with the Angel for a period before 1826? A later owner of the Angel said it was previously the Angel and Crown? When Mr Halford sold the Crown in 1826, did John Stanley acquire the Angel? We know he purchased it before 1834, as he had leased it to a farmer before that date. Where was the Bell and Crown, known to have existed from 1797 to 1814?

The 1882 deeds show the land and property that belonged to the 6th Earl Lord Coventry, which had been part of Crown, was taken up by the charity set up in the will of Thomas Hodges 1686 to support a charity school for poor boys. This land became the playground of the National School. As for the building, which appears to have been renamed Eadburgha Hall, before 1899, it became the village reading rooms[155] which opened 10 am-10 pm, it was also a meeting place for the WI, and described as the Working Men's Institute in 1985 deed. A conveyance dated 6 June 1906 identifies the land to the immediate east of Tudor House is owned by the Charity Trustees. In 1985 Henry Keil purchased Eadburgha Hall and renamed it Eadburgha House. It became one of his showrooms as part of his internationally renowned antique business. After 2008 it became offices, home to a

---

155. Bennetts Business Directory 1899

leadership training company, then a health and wellbeing centre. In 2022 it was put up for sale.

The hypothesis proposed, given the lack of Crown Inn records, the Bell Inn's story 1793-1820, the sale particulars of the Crown in 1826 and the Bell and Crown records between 1797 to 1814 and its sale in 1855, is as follows:

The Hypothesis concerning the Angel, Bell and Crown and Crown

Lord Coventry's stables became an Inn, the Crown, in 1744. It remained in his ownership up to the local Inclosure Act 1771. After the death of Ann Cormell in 1740, her daughters and their husbands oversaw the running of the Angel Inn. Later they saw an advantage in starting discussions concerning a partnership between the Angel and the Crown. At that time, Lord Coventry divested himself of the freehold of the Crown. The association existed between 1771 and 1793. Together both properties accommodated the 15 beds and had more land, more stabling, more extensive ground floor accommodation, more kitchens, and parlours. This partnership enabled them to compete with the Bell and the Lygon, both large establishments.

The only mention of the Angel and Crown was by Samuel Paxton Carless, the Tudor House's owner, in 1891. Careless told Hissey, the travel writer,[156] that Tudor House's building was previously the Angel and Crown.

When the Bell ceased trading or hardly traded as an Inn after Mr Smith purchased it due to his poor management Mrs Smith repurposed it. As the Bell had a better reputation than the Angel or the Crown, circa 1793, the partnership purchased the Bell licence and called the Angel and Crown the Bell and Crown. Mary Davies, wife of Richard,

---

156. John James Hissey, *Travels around England in a Dog Cart, and Leisurely Tour in England,* MacMillan, and Co, Ltd 1913

innkeeper of the Bell until the death of her husband in 1790, became the innkeeper of the Bell and Crown.

The Bell and Crown ran successfully though perhaps not cleverly, until, in 1820, the Bell was sold to the young Ashwins who wished to purchase back its licence. The Trust took advantage of the request, sold the licence back to the Bell, and then sold the Angel to John Stanley. This scenario fits with a lease with a local farmer for fourteen years, renewable in 1834.

The Crown traded on in its original name for a few years, but when all the coaches returned to the Bell in 1825, the Mail coach, the Aurora, the Telegraph, the battle was lost, the Crown was not sustainable. So, Mr Halford decided to sell the Crown and go abroad in 1826.

In 1840, Worcestershire trade directories confirmed all three, the Angel, Crown and Bell and Crown, had ceased trading. Despite surviving 160 years of trading in one guise or another.

The purchaser of the Crown in 1826 probably carried on a business until 1855. At that point, the plans to build a National School next door would have had to be considered. It would have been clear that the construction of the school and the actual prospect of a school next door would impact future trade, so the Bell and Crown was sold. The end of the Bell and Crown occurred on 4 June 1855, when the Bell was the location for the auction of the Bell and Crown;[157] its stables, coach houses and outbuildings were in the occupation of George Cooke. In 1882 the old Crown building and its land were owned by

---

157. Staffordshire Advertiser, for a valuable FREEHOLD PROPERTY, BROADWAY, Worcestershire. TO be SOLD by AUCTION by Mr. WILLDER, Monday,4th June 1855, at four o'clock in the afternoon, at the BELL INN. BROADWAY aforesaid, the following or such other lots as may be agreed upon at the time of sale and subject such conditions will then be produced: Lot 1. All that freehold property, known as the BELL AND CROWN INN, in Broadway in the county of Worcester, comprising the inn and premises, together with the stables, coach houses, outbuildings and garden, and other conveniences, situate in the centre of the village, and now in occupation Mr. George Cooke.

the Charity Trustees, and the building was renamed Eadburgha Hall. There appears to have been from the mid 19th Century a 'paternal' movement to educate the working classes; this Hall associated with St Eadburgha's Church became the village reading rooms. Representatives of the parish council, Thomas Hodges's Trustees and the Church appear to have worked together. A legacy of £400, from a parishioner Elizabeth Wylie, to the Vicar and Churchwardens of St Michael's Church, and an endowment for a school for the poor, and the Thomas Hodges charity income, could be brought together. They could then use £259 13s 0d to build and sustain St Michael's National School, adjacent to the reading rooms, and use some of the old Crown lands as a playground for the school.

Even if the Bell won the day, the heyday of coaching was nearly over. Sadly, the contribution of mail and stage coaching to the local economy is rarely celebrated, and an understanding of the jobs lost was never appreciated. The number of passengers in England between 1795 – 1835 is estimated at over 10 million. By 1830, the future of land transport was clear; the railway would be faster, cheaper, and more comfortable. Those with one eye on the national picture would have noted the emerging trajectory and its potential impact on Broadway's way of life. Once again, the thriving village with a population of 1700 would have to reinvent itself.

Chapter 14
The Angel Inn becomes a Farmhouse and is renamed Tudor House, Circa 1820's

When the Angel, its building, gardens, stables, lands, and rights of way were purchased, around 1820, by John Stanley, he leased the property, allotments, parcels of land, and any rights or associated properties to local farmers, amongst which was William Bloxham and William Cotterill. We know William Cotterill leased the building at one point to Charles Ingles.

On 22 and 23 July 1834, the lease with William Cotterill was renewed for 14 years. Stanley,[158] his heirs and assignees provided a mortgage to Cotterill, secured by payments from Cotterill, his heirs, and assignees of £400, plus interest at five per cent. On 24 July 24, 1838, and on 21 March 1842, two further legal agreements were drawn up between Cotterill and Stanley to cover two additional loans of £200 to Cotterill at the same interest rate.

On Cotterill's death on 27 April 1843, his estate passed to his wife Elizabeth, as was the custom and law, and then to his son John. The letters of administration of the goods, rights and chattels of Elizabeth showed the debt to John Stanley was made up of the three different sums, the original £400, the first £200, and the second £200 plus an outstanding sum of interest to the value of £80. The final total stood at £890. Stanley subsequently requested payment from John

---

158. Deeds show John Stanley lived in one house now divided: 148 High Street and 150 High Street.

Cotterill, for his father's debt of £880, for some reason reducing the sum by £10.

At the request of John Cotterill, Stephen Averill, another local farmer and landowner, lent him the sum of £1350 to enable him to discharge his father's debt. The interest rate on this sum remained five per cent. The loan was secured on Elizabeth's entitlement to the various incomes from the property, allotments, and land in question; she graciously agreed that all her title and rights should be extinguished. John then duly paid his father's debt of £880 to John Stanley from the £1350 advance, leaving £470 for his or his mother's use.

An indenture dated 20 April 1844, between Stanley, timber merchant John Cotterill, of Moreton in Marsh, Elizabeth, widow of William Cotterill and Steven Averill followed. Averill was to use all the property and lands until the debt of £1350 plus interest was repaid. The interest was to be paid annually on 20 October. A further deed limited the lease to no more than 14 years. Both Stanley and Elizabeth Cotterill signed a covenant confirming they no longer had any interest in the estate to complete the arrangements. John also had to sign a covenant to keep the estate in good repair and pay the estate's annual insurance, £500, to the County Fire Officer. Both costs added a further burden to his debt to Steven Averill.

1881 deed [159] precisely described the farmhouse's location, so we can be quite sure it was the old Angel; it was situated in the centre of the village, had Broadway Street to the north, Broad Close to the south and a property formerly known as the Crown to the east.

_____

159. The 1881 deed in its text refers to all the transaction previously going back to John Cormell.

The deed specified exactly what Elizabeth Cotterill had sacrificed when she extinguished all her rights: the farmhouse, previously the Angel, now Tudor House, farmyards, barns, stables, gardens, nearby fields, and five allotments in Badsey; in total, she had relinquished just over thirty-four acres, three perches, and twelve roods.

A year later, on 7 July 1845, another deed was drawn up between John Cotterill and Steven Averill; Cotterill had borrowed a further £200. He now owed £1550 to Averill and seemed in his dealings to have thought paying the interest was enough. He overlooked a clause in Averill's deed that specified the power of sale only required three months' notice to Cotterill for him to repay the £1350. Seven years later, it was acted upon.

In August 1852, an additional agreement was drawn between Cotterill and Averill senior, which included the signature of Averill's nephew, Isaac. Whilst John was, as requested, paying all the interest, as and when it was due, and the account that was up to date, the loan itself was still outstanding. Sometime later, Averill senior called in the debt. He agreed to pay Cotterill £2,000 for the equity of redemption of the premises; the sum considered the value of the premises, which was more than the debt. After deducting the debt and interest, John's final receipt was only £450.

The premises, the estate, and all rights to Tudor House now fell to the use of Stephen Averill, Isaac Averill, and his heirs.

It is most likely at this juncture in the building's history it was in a poor state: it was probably tired and run down, having been tenanted for thirty years or more, by various farming families. It is reasonable to assume that busy farmers did not invest in a building they did not own. They did make some clumsy alterations but, fortunately, few; the few changes internally and externally, since the new build, between 1660 and 1664, meant the heritage of the building was not obscured.

A year after the 1858 photograph was taken, in August 1859, through Stephen Averill's will, the whole estate passed to his nephew Isaac Averill in trust for Stephen Averill's adopted daughter, Sarah. We can only presume that Isaac Averill had agreed to be guardian or advisor to Sarah on Stephen Averill's death.

Chapter 15
Broadway's declining fortunes, and improvements at Tudor House,
1860 - 1883

By this period, in other parts of the Country, the predictions and actual impact of the 1830's early discussions concerning steam-driven vehicles and railways were becoming a reality. The end of the road for coaching was imminent. Initially, there had been no recognition of the threat. But, sadly, just as the coaching came into its maturity: safety concerns were being addressed, coach design improvements were being balanced to match road improvements, and speed was being better managed, it was all about to end.

For a short period, those involved with stage and mail coaching embraced steam. Some companies even converted to steam; the Cheltenham to Gloucester steam stage coach ran for about 3,000 miles. However, the idea of steam coaches was soon undermined by the very operators who had come up with the idea. They charged steam stage coaches £2 at the turnpikes, whereas the horse-drawn stage coaches had been charged 2s, thus achieving a financial own goal.

In Broadway, as early as January 1843, it had been recommended that Broadway had a station on condition that Sir Thomas Winnington, Bart, as Lord of the Manor[160], granted the requisite land

---

160. Sir Francis Winnington 5th Baronet sold 400 acres of Broadway's 3360 acres, mainly West End Farm and Peasebrook, and the title Lord of the Manor in 1886. Records say it had been in his family for 70-80 years. The Lordship itself is a curious title having been taken up by Sheldon after Babington who purchased the land from Queen Mary in 1558 sold him a smaller part of his land in 1573/4. Anthony Daston's widow purchased 2960 acres through Babington's sale. *Source Habington, who knew Broadway well and tells of the distribution.* The history of the Lordship still requires research as the statement re the length of ownership is at odds with that outlined elsewhere. The remnant of the Manor of Broadway and the Lordship of the Manor were acquired by the Broadway Trust in January 1985.

for that purpose[161] to the county. Disappointingly for both the economy and wellbeing of the village, he refused. Broadway was not to get its station until 1904.

In England, some stage coaches ceased as early as 1831; the final death knell came in 1838 when an act was passed permitting mail to be carried on trains. Locally, early in 1845, the public was respectfully informed[162] of arrangements being concluded with his lordship, the Postmaster General '*A New ROYAL MAIL service will commence on Sunday, 19 inst. leaving the Star Office, Worcester, every Evening at Half-past Six via Pershore, Evesham, Chipping Norton, and Woodstock to Oxford to meet the Mail Train on the Great Western Railway*'.

In 1886[163] The Manor of Willersey and Broadway and the 400-acre estate, made up of West End Farm and Peasebrook, across which the railway could, would or should have run, land which the family had owned for 70 to 80 years, was eventually sold off by the next generation, Sir Thomas's son, Sir Francis Winnington.

Hundreds of people in Broadway depended on coaching to earn a living. The only people in the trade who survived were carriers, taking goods to the railways or carrying passengers to local towns or villages

---

161. Worcester Journal 5 January 1843.
162. Worcestershire Chronicle of Wednesday, 22 January 1845.
163. Cheltenham Examiner 29th September 1886.

Carriers waiting for their fares in Montpellier Cheltenham

The loss of coaching and the failure to secure a railway halt in Broadway would prove devastating; not only did residents and businesses have to get their mail to or from Evesham, but the village was plunged into a sharp economic decline. Its population fell dramatically in the following years, from 1700 to 600.

Many great and valuable houses in the village lost a considerable percentage of their worth. The Angel, however, had already become repurposed as Tudor House. Properties were sold in a spiral of auctions, presumably for low prices as people left; others offered them at low rents. Some languished in various states of disrepair, including Abbots Grange. The old summer palace of the Abbots of Pershore had struggled to find a role since the dissolution of the monasteries in 1539. Around 1820, before the passing of the Poor Law Amendment Act, workhouses were already being built to reduce the spiralling cost of poor relief. In Broadway, the Grange found a role becoming the parish workhouse.

An early picture of Abbot's Grange said to be circa 1850

The Poor Law of 1934 ensured all relief only went to the workhouse. It was passed to ensure only the destitute qualified. It aimed to hide away and deter able-bodied paupers, to take them off the streets, and encourage hard work so that the poor never found themselves in a workhouse, a place known for meaningless daily drudgery and deprivation. In addition, the Authorities thought the workhouse would reduce the cost to the parish of supporting the poor.

It was a national failure, a flawed policy, verging on the inhuman, which inflicted untold misery and did little to reduce costs to the parish, but it did take the suffering poor out of sight. Now, in Broadway, as in other towns and villages, from the mid 19th Century, the loss of coaching and its associated trades was so devastating and the degree of desolation and poverty so extreme it could no longer be hidden away. Poverty was now evident, stark on Broadway's broad wide street, out in the open.

Slowly the village, its population much depleted, recovered. By 1875 the Grange was no longer a workhouse, and the parish had returned to its previous, less harsh way of addressing its incumbent poor. In the following century, clearances[164] would move them to industrial centres, but that is another story to be told.

24 July 1882, Isaac and Sarah Averill sold the property previously known as the Angel to Plaxton Samuel Carless, a gentleman from Middlesex. The sketch attached to the deeds identified the inn and its associated lands: the original building, a building to the west, and a stable at the rear, plus the footpath running to the west of the curtilage. The route in front of the building was named Broadway Street, just as it was on the Award map in 1771. It also detailed the Averill family were owners of land to the south and west of the footpath, and school charity trustees were landowners to the east.

Soon after his purchase Carless leased the house to George Bengough Hudson, previously of Bricklehampton Court, a property between Evesham and Pershore. We know little of Hudson other than he was the son of Henry Hudson of Cheltenham, who had been involved with insurance or reinsurance. He had married twice and was a keen huntsman who liked to say, '*he would never live out of sight of Bredon Hill*.'[165]

No longer a farmhouse, Tudor House presented itself as a gentleman's residence for the short period of Hudson's tenancy before his death in 1883. Hudson was buried in Wick Churchyard.

---

157. Living History direct from a contributor.
165. Unknown author, page of a book, Hudson of Wick, Page 212

George Hudson on the steps of Tudor House, circa 1882. The large buttress wall to the right appears to be supporting the whole wall of the original building.

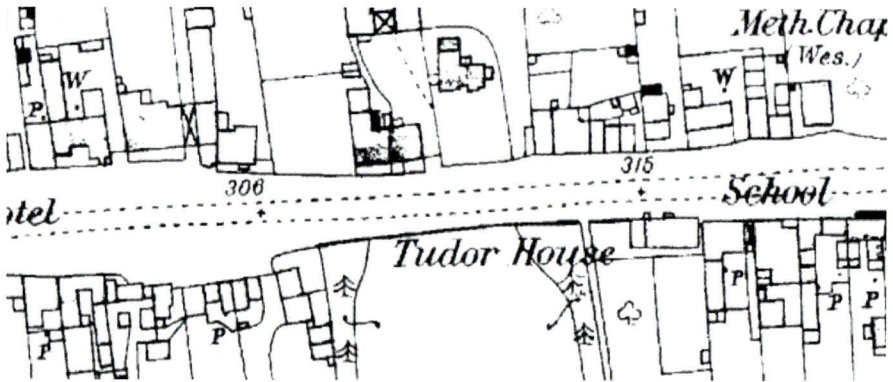

Tudor House around 1880 showing a small side extension behind the wall

After Hudson died in 1883, Carless set about organising the rebuilding of Tudor House's extension. By 1887, the buttress and small extension to the west had been replaced by a substantial new building, with a passageway to the rear of the property located on the east of the extension. The Angel, Tudor House, was like a caterpillar, morphing from its rustic external appearance as a farmhouse to a more attractive much-improved gentleman's residence.

Paxton Samuel Carless's investment sometime between the end of 1883 and 1887

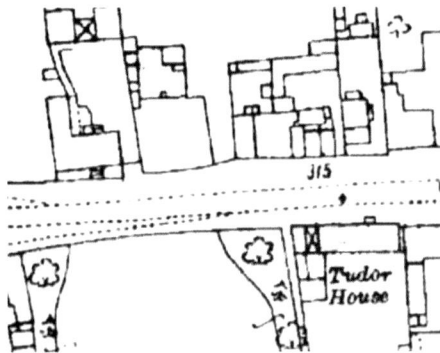

The new extension with its passageway is shown on a map dated 1900

This brand-new extension, added between 1883 and 1887, was evident in the photographs of Broadway's celebrations of Queen Victoria's 40th Jubilee.

Queen Victoria's 40th Jubilee in 1887
The school children from the National School, next bit one building up the High Street, joining in the celebrations

Shocking as Broadway's poverty was when coaching ended when one door closes, another often opens. As the village became a backwater, a rural idyll where large properties could be rented for low prices, it caught the attention of a very different sector of society; Broadway was set to become celebrated for its heritage, culture, and countryside.

The catalyst for this change, in 1867, was the renting of Broadway Tower to the pre-Raphaelite, designer, writer, and craftsman William Morris (1834-1896),[166] Edward Burne-Jones (1833-1898), and Gabriel Dante Rossetti (1828-1882). Seeking relief from city landscapes, the

---

166. Morris used the Tower as a studio and printing works. His time at the Tower inspired him to establish the Society for the Protection of Ancient Buildings in 1877.

three found their way to Broadway due to a lifelong friendship[167] between Cormell Price (1835-1910) and Edward Burne-Jones. Birmingham born Price had leased Broadway Tower[168]four years earlier, in 1863.

All three men were in harmony with the views of John Ruskin (1819 - 1900),[169] one of the first environmentalists to argue passionately against the destruction of nature and its beauties by the juggernaut called the Industrial Revolution. Broadway post-coaching offered a stark contrast to the ever increasingly populated, disturbed, and environmentally challenged industrial cities.

In 1885, the change was enhanced when the American painter, illustrator, writer and muralist, Francis D Millet (1846-1912),[170] Frank to his friends, was persuaded by Laurence Hutton, a friend of William Morris and Edward Burne-Jones, to move to Broadway. That year he rented Farnham House for the summer month[171] , taking full advantage of its low rent, good sized rooms with good light that could be used as studios, and ample living arrangements to accommodate and entertain umpteen guests. London in the summer was an unhealthy prospect. Not long before this period, Cholera had taken its toll. The city had only just addressed its need for a modern sewage system.

From this first summer onwards, history recounts the interestingly interwoven lives of more than 30 invited guests who visited intermittently, friends of the Millets, attracted to the peace and rurality of the village to live, work, and play together in the late 19th

---

167. Price and Burne-Jones had both attended the prestigious King Edward's School, Birmingham, founded in 1552. Price became the first headmaster of the United Services College at Westward Ho.
168. From Thomas Phillips, the renowned bibliographer who lived at Middle Hill.
169. Writer, philosopher, art critic, painter, poet of the period.
170. Sadly, he was one of the passengers who died when the Titanic sank in 1912.
171. It was also wise to leave London and other large cities in summer when diseases like cholera ran at their highest. The last major outbreak was 1866 and the sewage system was completed 1870.

Century: John Singer Sargent, Henry James, Edwin Austin Abbey, Alfred Parsons J. M. Barrie….

In 1890, the charismatic Mary Anderson (1859-1940), an eminent Shakespearian stage actor married to Antonio Fernando de Navarro (1860–1932), a fellow American, a barrister of Basque extraction, and Papal Privy Chamberlain of the Sword and Cape purchased settled at Court Farm in the upper part of Broadway High Street. The couple's musical interests and love of the arts made her a natural hostess for many of the soirees and events in Broadway, joining and complementing the high jinks of Broadway's Arts Colony. She, too, was a magnet attracting a range of literary and artistic guests, including Elgar.

There is no doubt that the establishment of the Broadway Artist Colony helped put Broadway on the map once again. In the early 20th Century, early shoots of national and international tourism blossomed due to a combination of factors and people: the heritage offers of Broadway's ancient High Street, its position on the Cotswold Way, the forward-thinking Sydney Russell who turned a what had become a mere beerhouse to a country house hotel, the Lygon Arms, and encouraged the new motoring traveller, its place as a centre for design, art and antiques.

The village was on the up. On 30th November 1899, Alderman Issac Averill, ex County Councillor, at the annual rent dinner at the Swan, for specific tenants, was clear[172] *"As far as he could see, the trade was very good, and he hoped it would continue so. Although as a nation we were in the midst of a venous war,[173] which involved a great sacrifice of life and money, he had no doubt all would come right in time."*

---

172. Evesham Standard & West Midland Observer - Saturday 02 December 1899
173. The Boer War 1899-1902

In 1902 Phil May[174] (1864 - 1903), the prolific and exuberant caricaturist known for his kind wit, and economy of line, just before humorously captured the change from the old ways to the new, a recovered and evolving Broadway.

Drawn by Philip William May caricaturist, and political satirist for Punch, a visitor to the Artist's Colony

The caricature depicts old rurality, jostling with modernity; the donkey, pigs and geese, old lady, carts, and waggons sit alongside the maid, the elegant lady and new-fangled motor vehicle. Carriers

---

174. Phil May died of tuberculosis, a condition he suffered from since childhood, at the young age of 39.

but no stage or mail coaches are depicted. In 1906 the change in Broadway between 1850 and 1905 was captured, this time in prose, by Charles G Harper.[175]

> *"Let us then imagine ourselves at Broadway, in Worcestershire and at the 'Lygon Arms' there. The village, still somewhat remote from railways, was once an important place on the London and Worcester Road, and its long, three-quarter-mile street is really as broad as its name implies; but since the disappearance of the coaches it has ceased to be the busy stage it once was, and has become, in the familiar ironic way of fortune, a haven of rest and quiet for those who are weary of the busy world; a home of artists amid the apple-orchards of the Vale of Evesham; a slumberous place of old gabled houses, with mullioned and transomed windows and old-time vanities of architectural enrichment; for this is a district of fine building-stone, and the old craftsmen were not slow to take advantage of their material, in the artistic sort."*

Charles G Harper: *The Old Inns of Old England, Volume II, A Picturesque Account of the Ancient and Storied Hostelries of Our Own Country*, London, Chapman & Hall Ltd, 1906.

What Harper did not mention when he wrote the quote above was that the railway did, in 1904, finally reach Broadway, bringing with it a new optimism, new residents, and new businesses.

Before we move further into the 20th Century, a firsthand account of the Angel in 1891, now Tudor House, tells us more of Paxton Samuel Carless and Tudor House….

Chapter 16.
James John Hissey's visit to Paxton Carless at Tudor House, previously an Inn, 1891

Broadway High Street, called Broadway Street, early 20th Century

Despite a couple of inaccuracies, the writings of James John Hissey,[176] in his book, Across England in a Dog Cart,[177] are a delightful first-hand account of his conversations with Paxton Carless in 1891 about the Angel.

Hissey had arrived in Broadway and alighted on a fine Elizabethan house in its main street, with three great gables in front. Over one of the bay mullions, he observed the date 1659 cut into the stone on a shield to the east and 1660 A.D. on a shield to the west, the same

---

176 James, John Hissey, Travels in a Dog Cart, Richard Bentley, 1st Edition 1891
177. Dog carts became illegal in the early 20th Century

shields barely visible today. 1659-60 referred to the build period during the Restoration period, following the Civil War.

Hissey's mention of an Elizabethan house was undoubtedly an assumption, as the property was named Tudor House. But, unlike some buildings located in the core of Broadway, Tudor House, previously the Angel, shows no signs of foundations or heritage features that imply Tudor origins or a Tudor conversion. Instead, the name may well have been first used when it became a farmhouse around 1820.

It is quite understandable that when the property's purpose changes, the owner might well wish to distance the property from its original use and ensure his tenants were not bothered by weary travellers. For example, in the golden age of coaching 1797-1820, stage and mail coaches ran, and inns were at their most lively, in part hectic, and sometimes notorious.

Some early photographs, late 19th Century, refer to the property as The Olde Tudor House, hinting of the Tudor period, implying a more ancient but unevidenced pedigree.

YE OLDE TUDOR HOUSE, BROADWAY.

A village postcard, date unknown, perpetuating the myth of a Tudor connection.

Nikolaus Pevsner[178] (1902-1983), known for his 46-volume series of county-by-county guides 'The Buildings of England (1951–74),' underlined that the building was constructed around 1659-60 and was assuredly of a period after the Stuarts succeeded the Tudors.

It is feasible that the name was chosen in the 19th Century because there had been an earlier 15th Century Tudor house or cottage on the site, which might have given way to the building. The building's proximity to other Elizabethan properties supports that theory: Tudor Cottage is opposite Tudor House, Mellowstones, 138 High Street, was part of the dowry of Catherine Parr on her second marriage,[179] 69 High Street, on the same side as Tudor House, only three properties away, still, has visible elements remaining of a Tudor building both internally and at the rear, and the weaver's

---

[178]. Pevsner, Nikolaus, *The Buildings of England*, Penguin Books, 1951.
[179]. Henry VIII's sixth and last wife who remarried after his death. She was a member of the Parr family of Sudeley Castle.

cottages in the upper area of the High Street are known as Elizabethan cottages.

Whilst photographing the outside of the building, Hissey met the owner, Paxton Carless, and arranged to visit the house. We learn from Hissey that Carless was a keen driver and had himself driven over 16,000 miles of English roads – an excellent achievement at that time. Hissey notes Carless had purchased the house on one of his trips.

Carless told Hissey that the old house was a former inn known as the Angel and Crown. An earlier chapter puts forward a hypothesis about this house and neighbouring properties to the east covering the period 1744 to 1855; part of the hypothesis supports this being the case. Apart from this one reference, extensive research has not yet revealed in any documents, deeds, wills, or newspapers referring to the Angel and Crown in Broadway. However, as discussed in earlier chapters, there are several references to the Bell and Crown.

Hissey also, following his meeting with Carless, writes, 'here at the Angel and Crown, Charles on his retreat from Evesham…….' [180] suggesting Charles II visited the Angel. He overlooks the fact that the building was not built until after the Civil War. Evidence[181] supports Charles II passing through Broadway and Evesham ten years or so before the inn was built. The honour of a visit to a Broadway house by the King is associated with the Savage family, owners of the 'Great Farme' demolished around 1773, located near St Eadburgha's just along from Bury End.[182] However, James I's horses were changed at the Angel around 1786.[183] Carless may have been mistaken as to which King had visited the property when it was an Inn.

---

180. 1644, destroying the bridge that was their lifeline for trade
181. Laird. *A Topographical and Historical Description of the County of Worcester*, Sherwood, Neely, and Jones, Paternoster Row; and George Cowie and Co. 1814.
182. A historic area of Broadway dating back to the Anglo Saxons if not before, before the old church, on a road now called Snowshill Road.
183. The overseers account in the Broadway Parish record, when they settle with Francis Phipps a debt related to livery expenses associated with of James I on his visit, a year before he abdicated.

One fascinating nugget from Hissey's first-hand account was that the old Parlour, either the main room on the ground floor or the sizeable old kitchen, had, at the time of the visit, hosted a small tribute to the Inn's coaching days. Carless had started a small Museum! Hissey wrote of how Carless prided himself on a collection of pictures representing the coaching days and treasured old toll gate tickets. The gems of this collection were the painted panels from two coaches, George I, a mail coach, and the back panel of the Truro to Penzance stage coach.[184]

184. James, John Hissey, Travels in a Dog Cart, Richard Bentley, 1st Edition 1891.

Chapter 17
Tudor House, 1892-1907

On 20 July 1892, ten years after he purchased, refurbished, and improved Tudor House, Carless, wrote a will[185] leaving his house, lands, and effects to his wife Bertha Ann and his brother-in-law Sidney Martin, an accountant. Two days later, he died.

When his will was finally proven by the Registry of Her Majesty's High Court, after a long wrangle with Martin, Bertha returned to London to Hampstead and Martin to Ross-on-Wye. They were named as joint Trustees of the Estate.

The house was then joint tenanted for several years by the Reverend C. M. Dix, who also gave his address as the Oratory, Edgbaston, and a Dr Windle[186]. They were not just second homeowners; both wrote to the local council in 1892 as passionate objectors to a local plan to pave Broadway's footways with blue brick. The County Council had given £90 towards repairing the paths. It was a heated topic in the village. Alderman Averill spoke for the proposal, but a petition signed by one hundred and twenty-three residents and a local vote for the use of local material and the use of local men won the day.

In 1904, Bertha and Sydney leased the property to Captain Jack Rodgers, a former Merchant Naval Officer from Liverpool. Known as John, he regularly travelled from Liverpool to Boston, USA, where he met his wife, the daughter of Irish immigrants, who had prospered in America. John's father and uncle were actor/managers in England. By the middle of the 19th Century, they had become proprietors of the Prince of Wales Theatre in Birmingham. Designed by Cranston, it opened its doors on 3 September 1856 with the "The Messiah". In

---

185. Will proven 3 September 1892.
186. Evesham Standard & West Midland Observer - Saturday 10 December 1892.

1861 Charles Dickens appeared there giving a reading of his "A Christmas Carol". In 1862 it became the Prince of Wales Operetta House, and in 1865, it was re-named Prince of Wales Theatre. On his father and uncle's death, John inherited the Theatre[187], which he very ably managed with his wife until his retirement, when he moved to Broadway.

John and his wife had two daughters, Ethel and Joan. The photograph below shows the girls with their children, Jack's grandchildren, in the garden of Tudor House, 1904 or 1905. The family refer to it as Old Tudor House, respectful of its antiquity.

From Left to right: Jack Ludlow, his mother Ethel Ludlow, nee Rogers, and Joan Winn holding her son Roger Winn, with Donald Ludlow, on Joseph, the donkey.

The donkey was a permanent feature to help pull the mower and donkey cart.

---

187. 9 April 1941, the Theatre was destroyed by German bombs when it received a direct hit on the auditorium. The building was demolished in 1987, and the new Civic and Conference Centre was built on the site: Symphony Hall.

Two of Jack's grandchildren were Lord Justice Roger Winn and Godfrey Winn, the author and journalist.

Jack Ludlow in the garden of the Old Tudor House circa 1904/5

On John's death several years later, his wife returned to America.

In October 1906, Bertha Carless and Martin conveyed the property to Arthur Labouchere (1842-1919) possibly, from the facial similarities, a younger brother Henry Labouchere (1831-1912) 1st Baron Taunton, who came from a wealthy Huguenot banking family, an English politician, writer, publisher, and theatre owner.

Print dated 1888, said to have been a fox hunter.

Arthur's signature is witnessed by a hotel proprietor: Percy Beer of the Princess Hotel, Bournemouth. Nine months later, on 6 June 1907, Arthur Labouchere sold the property for around £2,000 to 35-year-old Benjamin Martin Chandler, a wealthy American (1872-1948). A sketch of the location of the premises is on the deed. In this document, we learn that the adopted daughter of Stephen Averill, Sarah, became the wife of his nephew Isaac after Stephen's death.

After years of neglect and partial improvement, the property was about to enter a new adventure, not a renovation but a complete refurbishment. Benjamin Chandler was just the type of owner the sad, somewhat dilapidated building, previously the Angel, now Tudor House, needed.

The House in 1906 before its refurbishment by the Arts and Crafts architect, CE Mallows in 1909, the child may be Jack Ludlow, the gentleman Jack Rogers.

Chapter 18
Further investment - a gentleman's residence 1907-1914

Ben Chandler in his car (Chipping Camden 1908)

Chandler, born in 1872, came from a prosperous family, early North American settlers whose roots traced back to 1673. They had arrived in Boston as immigrant farmers and by the late 19th Century had become owners of the Amoskeag National Bank, based in Manchester, New Hampshire.[188]

He had inherited his wealth from his father, so he had the means to bring the property back to life. After attending Harvard University, he arrived in England in the first years of the 20th Century, drawn by the Arts and Crafts movement. He initially built a house for himself, known as the yellow house, in Buckland, Betchworth, near Dorking but following in the tracks of the many wealthy, cultured Americans, who favoured Broadway as their goal, soon departed for the North

---

188. This was one of the largest banks in the state of New Hampshire. It ceased trading in 1991 when it was absorbed into HN Bank Inc. of Manchester, a subsidiary of the Bank of Ireland in the USA. *New York Times Archives* 11 October 1991

Cotswolds. Here he decided to purchase and restore Tudor House for his wife, Frances Robbins, who hailed from an ancient yeoman family from nearby Weston sub-Edge.

He was unable to move in immediately, so he leased the property to Bernard Eyres Baldwyn on 21 October 1907, for a sum of money, subject to the vacation of the property on his payment to Baldwyn of £1200. Chandler had not sold the yellow house back in Betchworth, so it can be assumed the arrangement with Baldwyn provided a sort of bridging loan to supplement a down payment of £1000.

This temporary arrangement resulted in the building deteriorating even more from its poor state in 1907, as described by Alan Fea in his book,[189] *'The house was shut up, abandoned to the extent that nobody knew the ownership or whereabouts of the keys. No one went inside, and local people were speechless that anyone might wish to.'*

When Baldwyn died on 13 December 1909, the two executors of his will, dated 28 October 1908, Edward Righton and Oliver Hauxham, agreed with Chandler, 3 May 1910 to receive £1,000 instead of £1200 as previously agreed between Baldwyn and Chandler.

In 1909, Chandler set about remodelling Tudor House with the help of Charles Edward Mallows FRIBA (1864 – 1915), a sympathetic English landscape architect with an understanding of heritage. Mallows, known as C. E. Mallows, had been one of the first pupils, circa 1855, of William Flockhart (1850-1913), an inventive and original Scottish architect practising in London. Mallows was part of the Arts and Craft movement; it seems to have been Griggs who introduced Mallows to Chandler. Griggs had met Chandler in 1905

---

189. Allan Fea, *Nooks and Corners of Old England*, Secker, 1910.

when he made the drawings of Yellow House. Chandler supported Griggs in his brave acquisition of the fields at Dover's Hill, the backdrop to Campden.[190] There is evidence that Griggs was Mallow's pupil between 1896-98 when Griggs left architecture for art. Tudor House was the only house in the Cotswolds that Mallows worked on.

Chandler was also known for a passionate interest in cars; he built up quite a reputation with his two Mercedes sports cars, one for himself and one for his chauffeur, the same model Mercedes had sold to Kaiser Bill. It is said he owned the first car ever to be registered in Worcestershire, and there are those locally who have reported that, as a friend of Kenneth Graham, he might have been the model for Mr Toad in Graham's Wind in the Willows, published in 1908.

There is no doubt Chandler was frequently caught for speeding, but this was a period when the police, not 100% convinced about '*this car business*', focused heavily on laying traps for motorists. Motoring organisations evolved from the counter activity of volunteers who worked to challenge this practice. Nevertheless, so frequently was he caught for speeding that his reputation reached the pages of the Times Newspaper. F.L Griggs wrote to a friend about Chandler's driving 'Ben Chandler insisted on motoring us (in his silent and very fast car)…..'[191]

As the house was so dilapidated, Mallow's first task was to make it habitable, but in a way that respected the old property, leaving the main features intact. The main structure had remained unaltered for years, its interior had deteriorated, but only a few original features had disappeared. Previous owners or tenants had removed the old ground to the first-floor staircase, replacing it with a modern one of stone with a cast iron handrail. This had disfigured the hall and practically made that room, the Old Great Parlour, and the room

_____

191. Jerrold Northrop Moore, *F L Griggs (1876 - 1938): The Architecture of Dreams*, Clarendon Press, 1999. Page 156.

above, The Old Great Chamber, impossible as living rooms. Mallows set about having the monstrosity removed and replaced by a wooden staircase in a new position. A search was made for a staircase from another house. At first, rumours seemed to imply this was possible, but sadly it was not to be. Stepping up to the challenge Mallows designed the staircase in the building today. He based it on the upper staircase, which was still in its original location but then designed a much grander affair than the original 1660 staircase, which would have risen straight from the kitchen/lobby enabling passengers to enter the yard through the substantial external door to their chambers.

Photograph of the new staircase designed by Mallows for Tudor House in 1910

A 1907 layout shows that a second staircase had been added to the Great Parlour (occasionally called the Great Hall), significantly disturbing the room's proportions. The traces of this second staircase can still be found on the Great Parlour's ceiling today. Removing the second staircase in the ground floor main room would have been particularly pleasing. It restored the space to proportions in the original 1660 design, significantly improving the fireplace and the bay window setting.

The 1907 layout shows almost two separate areas, one entered from the street, the second from the yard at the rear. There appears to be no connection from the Hall area to the Parlour on the ground floor layout.

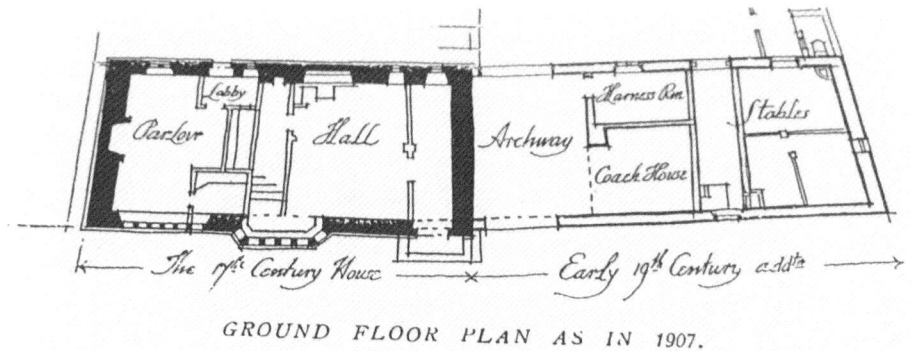

GROUND FLOOR PLAN AS IN 1907.

1907 Ground Floor layout before C.E. Mallow's restoration

The Haulway or Archway, part of Carless's new build between 1883 and 1887, is shown just to the west of the main house, next to a harness room and coach house room; that room could have housed smaller chaise, gigs, carts used by the property at that time.

Mallows' refurbishment work to the stable building to the west, which could historically have been space and shelter for coaching horses, would now stable personal, farm or hunting horses belonging to the tenants or past owners. He transformed the layout. The arch to the east moved further west of the building, and the eastern area was improved to include a kitchen and servant quarters, leading through to the improved stables, and more importantly, the housing for a motor car.

The 1907 first floor layout is in keeping with the building being a farmhouse for many years.

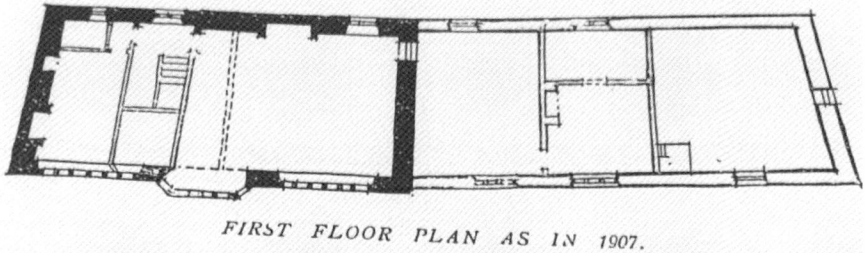

FIRST FLOOR PLAN AS IN 1907.

1907 First Floor layout before C.E. Mallow's restoration

The stone staircase and the staircase in the Great Parlour, called the Hall on the layout, led to several rooms; a door joined the main building to its extension, and steps addressed the level difference.

The main building's upper floors were partly in the roof.

When all the building work was finished, 10 September 1910, Country Life included a 5-page feature article on Tudor House, Broadway, Worcestershire, the residence of Mr B M Chandler.

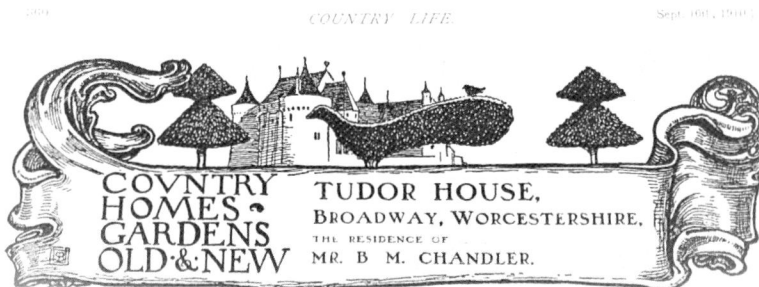

The article,[192] which focussed on the building's architecture, was accompanied by front and rear photographs of the Tudor House. It celebrated the Cotswolds as one of the country's best places to see 16th and 17th Century architecture. The progression from ecclesiastical architecture, associated with wool growing and wool weaving, to outbursts of Elizabethan and Jacobean architecture, then late gothic and the pure Palladian influences, in some places, that seemed to have been arrested in the 18th Century, was highlighted.

The article commended quality, the previous excellent apprentice schemes, and the importance of stonemasons and stone to the area. Stone quarried in the [193]Cotswolds contributed significantly to the work of Wren and Vanbrugh. In addition, the Cotswold stone had a prominent role in rebuilding London after the great fire in 1666.

The Country Life article celebrated Chandler's dedication to employing an architect who would retain the old and partly obscured features. Then it went on to lament that the railway coming to Broadway had bought with it 'the Jerry-built villa' but stated, fortunately, clustered near the station. Finally, the article mentions there had been a call when they were being built, in 1905, for any alterations and additions to follow the ancient form rigidly.

Two quotes in the magazine summed up the impact of Chandler's changes in 1909-1910. The changes *"once more made a long-ill-used house worthy of the days of its origins"* and *"the structure itself has never been seriously tampered with, but the interior had been somewhat drastically treated at a bad moment."*

Concerning the nondescript building to the west, the old archway, coach house and rooms, Country Life, had no information to appreciate its earlier history. They saw only the latest change, of 1887, so were dismissive, deeming rightly the extension was of no

_____

192. Author's own copy.
193. Ibid.

great age, unaware of this part of the property's roller-coaster existence since it was described in Phipps 1673 inventory.

Overall, Mallow's upgrade was a world away from the 1907 farmhouse; the owner was complimented for the interior, showing restraint, not being showy, the walls and ceilings whitewashed. The brown panelling of today was added twenty to thirty years later by a later owner.

The magazine shows the old Great Parlour on the ground floor, a comfortable living room, was going to be a dining room, served by the new kitchen with its scully[194] in the extension. Interestingly the furniture in the photographs of this room was 16th and 17[th]Century.

THE DINING-ROOM.

The Great Parlour, in 1910, on the ground floor showing curtaining rather than panelling

---

194. scullery is the term used to day

The Great Parlour in 2008 when H.W.Keil Ltd ran the building as an antique showroom

The Fireplace in the Great Parlour on the Ground Floor 2020

The article ends with yet another cry, within its text, to keep the old fine building traditions and resist the evil days of jerry-building; it was not dissimilar in tone and content from those leading locally to manage planning in Broadway today.

A valuable aspect of the article was the ground and first-floor layouts of the house in 1910, which could be compared to 1907.

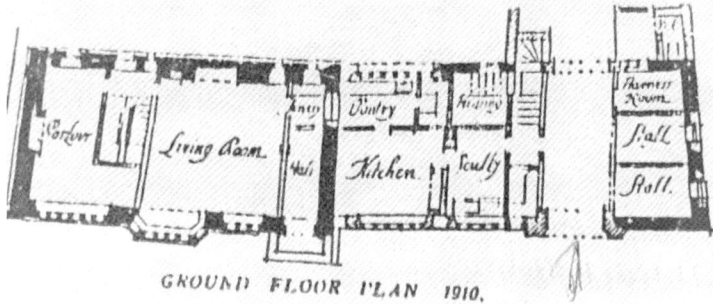

GROUND FLOOR PLAN 1910.

1910 Ground Floor layout after C.E. Mallow's restoration

The main changes on the ground floor were the enhancement of the main entrance, which looked to the High Street rather than the large coaching door that looked to the rear yard, and the repositioning of the passageway to the west, which allowed easy access to the Motor House.

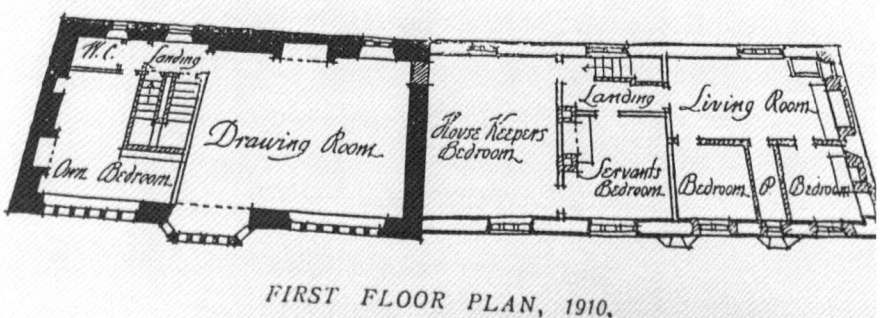

FIRST FLOOR PLAN, 1910.

1910 First Floor layout after C.E. Mallow's restoration

On the first floor, crucial elements are now the staircase, access to a water closet, connections to the housekeeper's room, the servant's room and two bedrooms for guests, each with their own living room rooms.

A LIVING-ROOM.

The Great Chamber on the first floor – is a living Room in 1910

The Great Chamber on the first floor – an antique showroom in 2008

Fireplace in the Great Chamber on the first floor, 2020

Chandler's daughter, Katherine, who lived at Tudor House, became a bookbinder and worked with the Arts and Crafts Bookbinder, Katharine Adams, whose workshop was in Eadburgha House, the next door to Tudor House, previously the Crown.

Adams would bind in leather, decorating in gold with little stamping tools: motifs, flowers, leaves, and dots. She would also fill panels of her designs with central motifs or lacelike patterns. Each book was monogrammed, with Katherine's mark.

Katherine Adams mark

Just after World War, I was declared, the Chandlers, several servants, including a governess, all of whom has lived at Tudor House, moved to Hathaway House in South Littleton. Why is not clarified, perhaps the proximity to the Honeybourne Station, a faster line to London, or greater isolation, either connected with the declaration of war, may have been the drivers behind this change?

Chapter 19
Home to a retired Civil Servant, society lady and the start of a business enterprise, 1914-1935

In 1914, roughly two months after the First World War was declared, Chandler sold the house to Sir Richard Amplett Lamb K.C.S.I. C.S.I. C.I.E. Indian Civil Service, an Ordinary Member and Vice-President of the Council of the Governor of Bombay. He had entered the Indian Civil Service in Bombay in 1877 as a forestry settlement officer, then rose to the position of Deputy Commissioner.

He lived at the house with his wife, Kathleen. Lamb, who had been educated at King Edward's Grammar School, Stourbridge

The indenture between Chandler, Dr George Hearthan, and Joseph Rawlings, Bank Manager and Lamb, confirms it was a mortgaged property.[195] On Sir Richard's death, 27 January 1923, his wife, Lady Kathleen, moved to London. Estate duty was administered on 8 November 1926. 15 December 1926 Lady Kathleen sold Tudor House to Mrs Elizabeth Galmour Arthur, of Mayfair. On the front of Tudor House are the neatly carved initials RL, thought to have been added by Lamb or his widow.

Discrete but formal lettering, carved on the front of Tudor House

---

195. Record copy in author's archives.

Little is known of Elizabeth Glamour Arthur at this point. On 10 April 1935, Elizabeth sold the house for £1,050 to a gentleman well known in Broadway, the antique dealer Henry William Keil, Leeds House, High Street, Broadway. The sale deed[196] described Tudor House as a dwelling with a stable, motor house, yards and gardens, outbuildings adjoining and belonging, formerly a farmhouse.' It is located 'nearly in the centre ……… and having the street or highway leading through Broadway to London on the south, in part by a Close now or lately called "Broad Close.' It gives new information about the Crown; '*on the south and west after it ceased to be an Inn*'. The deed refers to a messuage formerly known as the "*Crown Inn*", lately occupied by the "*Working Men's*" Institute and historically by the Managers of the National Schools as a playground, but now of late the property of and occupied by Mrs L A Keyle on the east.

Leeds House was Henry Keil's first showroom in Broadway.

Leeds House, in the upper section of the High Street

196. Record copy in author's archives, dated 10 April 1935.

Chapter 20
Tudor House, H. W. Keil Ltd, one of the world's leading antique furniture businesses, 1935- 2008

Some of the credit for the success of Broadway, the village, in the 20th Century can be attributed to Henry William Keil, known to many locally as Bill.

His father, J W Keil, born in Middlesex, South Hackney, roughly two miles from Shoreditch, was a carpenter who became a master cabinet maker at forty-four. Shoreditch was the home of the furniture-making industry from about 1820 to the late 19th or very early 20th Century.[197] Henry was born in 1900, one of five children in Camberley, Surrey.

At the outbreak of War in 1914, he volunteered for war work. He was placed as an apprentice in the experimental section of the Royal Aircraft Establishment at Farnborough as a pattern maker. Later, in 1917, having gained a senior apprenticeship position, he was chosen for pilot training in the Royal Flying Core. When he became medically unfit, Keil transferred to the Young Soldiers' Battalion of the 5th Middlesex serving in France until wounded and discharged.

After the war in 1919, like many returning soldiers, he wanted to build his own career paths. He took advantage of the additional educational opportunities offered by the authorities. He was awarded a scholarship from 1919 -1923 to

---

197. Shoreditch, known for Elizabethan theatre, was in 1800 a mere 640 acres. It grew faster than any other London Parish from the 1800s. By 1851 it had 130,000 inhabitants. The south of the parish was the centre for the furniture trade and other artisans.
http://www.bonsonhistory.co.uk/html/hoxton___shoreditch and a visit to Geffrye Museum.

study design and technology, linked to woodwork, at Guildford School of Art[199] and later the Victoria and Albert Museum. He won several prizes in his latter days at college and valuable work experience: first place and a silver medal in his final examination at the London Institute City and Guilds. He also won bronze in the Royal Society of Arts in Design and Craftmanship assessment. Between 1923 and 1927, Keil lectured in woodwork technology and became a Fellow of the Royal Society of Arts.

He married Violet Webb in Hampshire in April 1925, then moved to the High Street Broadway in 1926 to join Gordon Russell, son of Sydney Russell, owner of the Lygon Arms, who had started a furniture design business after the war. Keil ran the antique furniture division from the Russell workshops; its success in no small part was his ability to engage with the American clients. Autumn 1929, the Wall Street crash, which started in September and went into late October, severely impacted Russell's business. As Sales Manager, just twenty-nine, Keil set sail from Liverpool, 19 October 1929, on the Adriatic, the White Star Line, bound for New York to address the business challenges. Despite his valiant efforts, he could not avoid the collapse of Russell's international business and the closure of the antique division in 1931.

Undaunted, in 1932, Keil established his own firm selling English Furniture and Antiques, specialising particularly in oak and walnut furniture of the 16th, 17th and 18th Centuries. His initial workbench training and his American contacts served him well. Public records show Keil as head of the family, a furniture proprietor, living at Leeds House, Broadway, with his wife Violet and their daughter Joyce, in 1931-32. As the businesses grew, Henry 'Bill' and his wife Violet, known locally as 'Poppy', purchased the larger premises of Tudor House in April 1935 to give him scope to expand his business further. Tudor House became his showrooms; its many rooms were carefully

---

199. Guildford was known for its woodwork courses during this period.

arranged with fine furniture of all periods, each piece carefully displayed and organised for quality and colour.

Although his first love was oak furniture dating from the 17th Century, he had an exceptional eye for walnut furniture, each piece being chosen for colour and form. For the collector, there were outstanding examples, the finest selection of 17th and 18th Century furniture in the West of England.

To accommodate the changes, only a few internal alterations were made to the building: the removal of ceilings in some rooms to reveal the beams and the addition of panelling in the main rooms. The panelling is not authentic to the building's original period, it suited the building, adding warmth to protect the pieces and keeping damp out. Scrutiny of the panelling in the dining room of the Lygon Arms, adjacent to the Great Hall, shows that it had been added around 1910.

Bill's son Peter advised, *"Finding panelling in a period when larger houses were being decommissioned, and large areas in cities were being 'modernised' was more straightforward than it might seem. In addition, the cost was lower than we might imagine today."*

The only other changes were the creation of an office in the old kitchen and the repositioning of the staircase in the extension in 1952, from the rear, near the new cellar, to its current position.

The trade spoke highly of him, describing him as a consummate salesman. He was spoken of occasionally as slightly wary of the other members of the trade but charming, gracious, and willing to impart his extensive knowledge if you had a similar passion to his.

John told me his father advised him of a particularly 'important' sale of antiques coming up in Wales. John rose early to make the two- or three-hour journey to get down to the auction house before other dealers arrived, only to find his father had already purchased the best items. A life lesson for John from his father.

A resident in the High Street who knew Keil told me recently, "there was no side to Bill; he was straightforward, but when he talked to you about antiques, the object of his attention turned to gold in front of your eyes. He had a marvellous way about him."

Recently a previous junior member of Bill's staff commented on the degree to which Bill asked him to arrange and rearrange the furniture in the showrooms under his watchful eye. "We polished the furniture on their hands and knees for many hours, a great way to study furniture and learn about both sorts of joints, mine and the furniture's", he added.

Tudor House, with its panelling, the photograph was taken around 1980

The Keil family subsequently acquired Broad Close across the street, which became their family home. The two boys, John and Peter would go on to make their successes in the antique world. Peter would speak of his childhood affectionately. He had memories of sitting in his pyjamas before bedtime, on the steps of the small balcony over the main room, listening and learning, as his parent's entertained friends and clients alike. [200]

Bill commissioned workshops for cabinet makers and a forge, blacksmith workshop in the Close behind his home. In addition, several ex-Gordon Russell employees joined the firm as antique restorers.

1958-1964 photographs of workshops and the forge

Mr Fred Dowdswell in the Forge   *Mr Alan Trinder working on a bureau.*

In part, thanks to his experience in the international sector of Gordon Russell's business, his network included international clientele and a royal customer, HRH the Duchess of York (later Queen Elizabeth, The Queen Mother). Her visit to his showroom in 1934 when she visited her aunt, Lady Maud Bowes-Lyon, of Orchard Farm,

---

200. Personal recollection.

High Street, which was reported in the Evesham Journal, 7 June, helped enhance his firm's already growing reputation.

Tudor House was assessed and graded II* and listed on 30 July 1959.[201]

In 1985, fifty years after establishing his businesses, H. W. Keil Ltd purchased 'Eadburgha Hall' now called Eadburgha House, thus bringing the old Crown Inn and Angel Inn together and acquiring more showroom space. The two buildings, Tudor House and Eadburgha House, remain in the same ownership today; the internal connection between the buildings was blocked off as late as 2012 when Tudor House became the Museum. A further chapter for the Keil buildings seems planned for 2022.

Eadburgha Hall, now Eadburgha House, photographed in the 1980s.

201. Historic England.org.uk, list entry, 1288137

In addition, the Keil's purchased the old National School building to the east of Eadburgha House.

A glimpse of Tudor House and Eadburgha Hall, taken from the old National School building in the 1940s

Bill Keil bought and sold other large properties in Broadway such as Barn House, 152 High Street, Farnham House and Russell House, Lower Green. He improved them but also shrewdly added covenants[202] to ensure these large properties could never become antique showrooms in the future.

Keil's stock showed quality and taste, as was evident in his many advertisements. They were an important feature of The Antique

---

202. Deeds Farnham House, Comments re Russell House.

Dealer and Collector's Guide of the '50s, '60s and '70s. In addition, his collection of designed drawings for ironwork, soft furnishings, and photographs of genres of antiques is possibly unrivalled.

His attraction for earlier pieces was clearly indicated by his collection, which was carefully displayed in his 'museum', an inner sanctum; he had acquired them over many years refusing to sell at any price. Later Peter, then John would continue their father's 'museum', an area within the shop. They both stayed true to their father's reluctance to sell their best items, keeping them where visitors could look and admire them but not buy.

On Bill's death in 1983, after 53 years of collecting and trading, Violet remained in Broad Close, and his many businesses passed to his two sons, John, and Peter, to add to their collection of successful businesses. Possibly foremost, Peter appeared to run the business in Broadway, and John, H. W. Keil (Cheltenham) Ltd, located at 129, The Promenade.

H W Keil's antique business in Broadway appeared to be run by Peter. When the District Council would not permit Broad Close, previously a family home now OKA, to be a showroom, he 'informally' extended the client an invitation to his home. Each floor of Broad Close housed exquisite antiques; each room was organised to reflect a different period on each of the four floors. A tour for favoured guests was an enchanting journey through time. [203]

True to their father's tradition, all the families' antique showrooms displayed the finest of their 17th and 18th Century oak and walnut furniture. Moreover, the significant reputation built up by their father grew; the antique galleries of H.W. Keil Ltd, whether in the Cotswolds or London, became destinations in themselves and Keil's wax polish was a firm favourite in many Broadway homes.

---

203. One of the author's personal memories.

Photograph of the building in the 1960s

When Peter tragically died in October 2007, when crossing an unlit[204] section of the High Street, close to his showrooms, the Broadway arm of H. W. Keil Ltd passed to John.

John set out to ensure that the ambition of his father that his 'museum' pieces be displayed in an actual Museum became a reality. He contacted the Ashmolean Museum in Oxford, an institution he knew well and regularly supported. A new adventure started, and today, many of these pieces are now via the Ashmolean Oxford and their support in the main room of Broadway's Museum and Art Gallery.

---

204. The lighting of the street, provided by the Horse and Hound public house, across the road from Tudor House, had not yet changed to wintertime that year.

Sadly in 2008, after seventy-eight years of trading, HW Keil's antique business in Broadway closed its doors for the last time.

Chapter 21
The Historic House becomes a Museum, 2008 - 2022

In August 2008, at the instigation of John Keil, tentative discussions teased out the feasibility of Tudor House, the building, becoming a museum. John approached Elizabeth Eyre[205], in her role as County Councillor for the Broadway Division, on Worcestershire County Council to discuss how the project could be taken forward. Together, as founding trustees, they widened the network to include the Director of the Ashmolean Museum, Christopher Brown.

Sometime later, Elizabeth approached a colleague and friend Geoffrey Bowman, an architect who lived at Pear Tree House, and John Painter, Chairman of Herefordshire, and Worcestershire Chamber of Commerce, to establish an initial steering committee.

Officers from Worcestershire County Council worked with the Fire Authority, English Heritage, and the District Council to check the condition of the property and its suitability to display loaned objects in appropriate period settings, its accessibility, and the many necessary health and safety and check the security arrangements, that would be required.

In May 2009, the building was offered to the initial four steering committee members by John Keil. At that point, the hard work to progress the concept from an inkling in John Keil's eye to a functional museum began in earnest: planning the required physical building changes, the planning permissions, and preparing the capital and revenue business cases. However, none of this could come to fruition without a fundraising plan and, more crucially, a programme of dynamic, active fundraising.

---

205. Author of the book.

Building on a planned one-off injection of £200,000 from the County Council, the project began to gain both local businesses and residents' support. As a result, grants were applied for, planning permission was granted, and a 50-year lease was negotiated.

Under Geoffrey Bowman's watchful eye, the building work began in earnest in 2010; adaptations were carried out from then until 2012, enabling the Museum to open in September 2013 as the Ashmolean Museum in Broadway. But, of course, none of this could have been achieved without the team's many hours of hard work committed to the project.

Such ventures are never plain sailing: substantial additional financial support was needed and generously given by John Keil, a robbery of irreplaceable silver items April 2015, causing concern to the Ashmolean, almost led to the closure of the museum, and the constant complications of raising funding when associated with the name Ashmolean necessitated a name change in 2017 to Broadway Museum and Art Gallery.

This book is dedicated to my co-founder, John Keil, who passed away in April 2015 and everyone who supported me from 2008 to 2021, to create Broadway's Museum and Art Gallery. Thanks to new colleagues invited to join the Trust in 2017, each with their specialist skills, the Museum continues to thrive. Good leadership is vital to sustainability.

It is also important to thank past trustees who have supported the venture through some tough, even dark days, the staff over the years, the many magnificent selfless volunteers, and finally, the museum's donors, friends, and benefactors.

The Angel, Tudor House, now moves forward in 2022 to a new chapter ……

Appendix 1.
Broadway Coaching Inns, Other Inns, Ale, Beer and Cider Houses, including Maltsters and Carriers

For most people in Broadway, life was tough until the 15th Century. Although it was less challenging than their forefathers, who were enslaved at times to conquerors or feudal lords, there was little leisure time except perhaps on market days, formal holidays, and church days.

The Bubonic Plague, or Black Death, reached England around June 1348[206] and the Midlands the following summer. It lasted until about 1350 and changed society from the bottom up; it was a silent revolution. When it was over, England had fewer people to work the fields. A surge of demands for a fairer society came from those remaining; this set of circumstances ensured change was brought about with minimum violence. It was no different in Broadway.

People then began to have extra time and earnings, which they could spend in the ale, beer or cider houses, taverns, and inns. In addition, these were public gathering places where you could see your neighbours and even hold events like weddings and wakes until laws were enacted to make such non-church religious events illegal.

There was a distinction between the offer of each house. An ale, beer or cider house was an ordinary home serving a homemade brew. If they provided lodging, it was likely to be a straw bed on the floor; occasionally, they provided food. Taverns or Inns were generally purpose-built. Taverns might only offer drink; inns would

---

[206] It arrived in England in June 1348 and by the spring of 1349 starting to ravage Wales and the Midlands. *Kevin Goodman, Disease, and Illness in the Black Country, Volume I, Medieval to Early Medieval, Bows, Blades and Battles Press 2020* and *www/bbc.c.uk/history/British/middle/ages/black/death.*

offer more rooms than a family would need and superior stabling. Inns also brewed ale, then beer and possibly wine, commonly drunk with water; the clarets of Bordeaux were part of a brisk trade with France.

Inns advertised their business with a sign hanging outside in common with other tradespeople of the period. Most of the population were illiterate; hence inn signs were often pictorial.

Taverns were drinking houses and would have been less popular, attracting some illicit criminal activity and barmaids that might pick up extra coin by engaging in 'certain' activities. Taverns encouraged gaming and drinking: cards, dice, and other table-top games. Bowling games and short-range archery could have been played in alleys nearby. It is feasible some clients paid their bills in kind, which suggests a black market in goods, and some innkeepers could have been moneylenders. Travellers from other towns were called foreigners and from other countries, as written in ale and beer house Parliamentary Acts,[207] were known as aliens. As a result, they fell under constant suspicion when, in fact, most were only going about their business.

Even with the picture not fully painted, we can see how stage and mail coaching came and went in Broadway, impacting those in associated trades, particularly the ale, beer, cider sellers and Innkeepers. There is a misplaced nostalgia when inns, stage and mail coaches are mentioned. Coaching was a necessity for most but uncomfortable, unpleasant, malodourous, to say the least, and could be dangerous. Innkeeping was hard work, exacerbated, rightly, by the constant stream of attempts, coercion, and legislation to control innkeepers' activities. A second appendix is intended to give the reader just a flavour of the Parliamentary Acts and regulations that challenged the innkeepers, many of whom we should remember had little or no formal education.

---

207. Appendix 2.

Broadway Coaching Inns, Other Inns, Beer Houses, Cider Houses, Maltsters and carriers

Based on research to date,[208] an ongoing project.

1. Hotels & Inns where stage or mail coaching took or possibly took place.

1490 The Whyte Harte, White Hart, now the Lygon Arms, High Street. The Lygon Arms is a composite building now embracing several old buildings and newer additions: a lower building once the home of the Dickens family, the core of the Inn, a medieval freeman's house to the rear, circa 1906 a building to the east known as Spencer's cottage, the Great Hall built in 1910, the kitchens added 1911, the larders and pantries, the garages for the 'new' motoring tourist and accommodation for their chauffeurs in 1926, the Lygon Arms Country Club and Spa in 1984, the Garden wing in 1960 and the Orchard Wing, which incorporated a conference room named the Edinburgh Room, in honour of its use when the Duke of Edinburgh toured the Gordon Russell Showrooms in 1968.

The Inn, originally the White Harte, became a hospitality provider in 1490 as evidenced by a 31-year conventual lease, [209] for an annual rent of £30 a year,[210] between the Abbot of Pershore, Lord of the

---

208. Local lists, books on Broadway's history, newspaper cuttings, John Morris's 1924 typed list. John Morris was a Broadway man, who had a retail outlet. There are still family members living in Broadway.
209. Relating or belonging to a convent.
210. £30 is roughly equal to £20,095 in 2017, (inflation 1.3%) Bank of England. source It would buy, roughly calculated, one of the following 21 horses, 78 cows, 272 stones of wool, 75 quarters of wheat and 1000 days labour of a skilled man. (National Archives Currency Converter 1270-2017).

Manor, and two under-tenants, Robert Handy and Robert Faulkes.[211] They or their assignees are to *'supply sufficient meat and drink, and bedding to the abbot's steward holding court there and six men with him, meat and litter for their horses, that is to say for a night and a day and other time during the said term.'* The assignee who provided this service was Thomas Whyte, of Whyte Hall, located near the Wool House.[212]

The Whyte (White) Hart was said to be owned by John Treavis in 1549, but recent research suggests William Sandbache sold it to John Treavis in 1613. William, the second Earl Beauchamp Lygon (1782-1823), purchased the Inn in 1820 and gave it his family name. It became the Lygon Arms. The first official record in which the White Hart is listed as "the Lygon Arms" is the 1841 census. The Inn has had a long tradition of providing post-horses and being a stop for carriers and private coaches. Later in history, stage coaches, mail coaches, and gigs stopped at the Inn. Dennick and Stevens ran stages from there. Of the four daily stages from Worcester to London and vice versa, several changed horses there: the Sovereign, Royal Mail, and Highflyer, commonly known as the Fly. In 1839 Charles Drury purchased the Inn and occupied it until his death in 1879. The Inn passed to his son Charles Richardson Drury who died in 1900. Sydney B Russell rescued the premises from its position as a run-down beer hall, owned by his employer, the brewing firm of Allsopp, in 1903. It remained connected to the Russell family for seventy-eight years until the last family member died in 1981. From 1981 to 1986, it remained in the safe hands of Donald Russell's successor and manager, Kirk Ritchie. Eventually, it moved into the more corporate world, being owned, and managed by the Savoy from 1986, Furlong Hotels from 2003, which became Dawnay Day 2005, Barcelo Hotels 2007, which rebadged itself as Puma Hotels 2008, then Hotel

---

211. The 1490 lease, which mentions Handy and Faulkes, confirms they had leased the premises before, 'as of old times.' Cited in *the Story of the Lygon Arms* Alison Ridley and Curtis F Garfield and confirmed by additional research by the author.

212. An older area in the Lygon Arms is possibly Broadway's Wool House used in trading.

Collection in the same year and is now in the more sustainable hands of London and Regional since 2016.

1660 – 1820 The Angel Inn, High Street, now Tudor House. The purpose-built stage coaching Inn, the subject of this book, ceased trading in its original name sometime in the early 19th Century. It was sold to a timber merchant before 1820 to become a farmhouse and was renamed Tudor House. In the late 19th Century, it was unsympathetically upgraded to be a gentleman's residence. In 1910, the building was completely renovated in a manner that retained the original character of the house whilst modernising it. In 1932, it became the showroom of a prestigious antique business. In September 2013, it opened its doors as Broadway Museum and Art Gallery. For most of its life as an Inn, it served as a stop for stage coaches rather than mail coaches. It now serves travellers in a different way.

Circa 1750 – 1850, The Fish Inn, Fish Hill, a coaching stop from the third quarter of the 18th Century to mid 19th Century. The original building seems to have been a summer house. Deeds linked to the land on which Farncombe Estate sits date back to 1560. The Brookes family owned it between 1720 and 1760; it then passed to another branch of the family, the Cotterells. The first building on the site of Farncombe House was an ox hall; the main house we see today was built by Sir John Cotterells in 1780, incorporating some small sections from 1681. It is unknown who built the summer house or when it was converted. Still, there is a strong possibility it was converted to an Inn when the road up Broadway Hill was rerouted, as The Fish Inn, Broadway is mentioned in the 1756 Act linked to the rerouting. This rerouting is thought to have impacted the profitability of the old Bell Inn, at the top of the High Street just before the turning circle, now Court Farm. British Listed Buildings suggest the Fish Inn stemmed from a summer house, which later became a public house around 1771. The listed building record highlights several late 19th Century additions to the property. 1771 ties back to changes due to the local land enclosures. It was mentioned as an Inn in 1814.[213] In 1829 Ralph Newman was victualler at the sign of the Fish, Broadway Hill.[214] Coaches stopped here to unhitch the extra horses needed to climb the hill, change horses, and water horses. It has been said that the lead horse in a team is called the Fish, hence the name of the Inn, but no evidence of that terminology has been found.

The 'old' Bell, 1727 -1773, is now part of Court Farm in the High Street. This Inn is suggested as a modest dwelling or small farmhouse that sprang up as an alehouse or beer sellers house on the road out of Broadway around 1727.[215] It reverted to Bell farmhouse[216] around 1770-1773 when its licence moved to the Bell Inn in the centre of Broadway. The change of route up Fish Hill and the opening of the Fish Inn is said to have impacted the old Bell's trade from 1771. The farmhouse was incorporated into Court Farm in the 20th Century.

1700–1760 The King's Arms, subsequently The Bell, now Picton House, **High Street,** is thought to have been built as a farmhouse in 1700 by the Stretch family using ashlar stone from the old Broadway Court after it was demolished in 1733. It was known to be a Tory house and may well have been called the George. It was said to have been renamed the Bell when the license from the old Bell moved to this premises after the Fish Inn opened on Broadway Hill.

Circa 1760 to 1867, the Bell Inn, now Picton House and Bell House, High Street. In 1770-1771 the Enclosure[217] Commissioners made the Bell their headquarters. In 1820 for a short time, the Aurora stopped here. In 1840 it was the calling house for the Monarch stage coach, where horses were changed until 1897. It had a magnificent signpost similar to that outside

---

213. *Laird A Topographical and Historical Description of the County of Worcester, Sherwood, Neely, and Jones, Paternoster Row; and George Cowie and Co. 1814.*

214. Worcester Journal 5 November 1829.

215. *John Morris' typed record 1924* is thought to have been a basis for Ballie's later publication.

216. Now incorporated into Court Farm.

217. The Act was spelt Inclosure

the Lygon Arms today. When the owner who purchased it in 1793 ran into financial difficulties, his wife, Mrs Smith, took in young ladies and ran the Bell as a ladies Academy.[218] in 1809. She acquired the property herself and ran it as a ladies Seminary from 1809 -1820. The subsequent owners, Mr and Mrs Ashwin, used the property as an Inn and a school. The Inn accommodated both stage and mail coaches, mid 18th Century as evidenced in the Gazetteer or Trade magazines. Finally, in 1867, Sir Thomas Phillips purchased the property and turned it into a private house. He organised the removal of the signpost.

1744 – 1793 The Crown, High Street. This old posting house with stables is thought originally to have been used as the stabling for the Coventry family, who had their own coaches. It is believed to have become a posting house in 1744 when the archway was added, and until 1771 may have traded in this name. At some point, it is **thought to have traded as the Bell and Crown, possibly from 1793 to 1820**, when the Bell Inn did not require its licence and may have been run by a landlady of some repute known as 'Queen Ann'. Numerous auctions took place at the inn between 1797 and 1818. The property continued to provide accommodation until it sold in 1855 but did not trade as a coaching Inn after 1826. It is later referred to as Eadburgha Hall or just the Reading Rooms to reflect its new role in the village. From 1985 it became a showroom for H. W. Keil Ltd antiques until Broadway's arm ceased in 2008. Subsequent tenants included then from 2008 a management company, and later a therapy centre. The property is now called Eadburgha House.

The Crown and Angel, High Street, the Crown, and the Angel may have combined for a brief period between 1771 and 1793 when the Angel was sold to John Stanley, the Timber merchant. However, only one reference has been found.

1794 -1820 Bell and Crown High Street, Eadburgha Hall, and part of the site of the National Schools built in 1856. The Crown and land to the east, school land, may have been used as an Inn, the Bell and Crown, when the Bell Inn was primarily a ladies academy/ladies seminary between 1793 and 1820. The Bell's Licence may have moved across the road for part of this period. A source[219] suggests the Bell and Crown had 15 bedrooms and extensive stables for 25 horses and grounds of two acres. This description would fit the size of the Crown; the extensive stabling at the Crown linked to the Coventry's and land to the east belonging to the Thomas Hodges School charity could be rented. The Angel may also have been linked to or supported the Crown or Bell and Crown for a short period, as mentioned by Samuel Paxton Carless in 1891, but we have no solid evidence. See hypothesis in the main book.

2. Other Inns, or accommodation providers, not thought to have ever been coaching Inns.

18th Century or before

1700- 1800, Abbots Grange (Priory) off Chapel, now Church Street. It possibly provided accommodation to travellers at some point. Abbots Grange is also a complex medieval building with timber-framed elements dating to the 14th Century, extended and altered over time. Post the monastery's dissolution locally in 1539, it may have provided hospitality in the early 17th to early 18th Century. Post-1820 but before 1875, it served as the parish workhouse, particularly after the 1834 Poor Act change of emphasis. In the late 1800s, the much-deteriorated priory was acquired by Frank Millet for studio space. With advice from William Morris, Millet gradually restored Abbots Grange. His finest work 'Between two fires' was painted in The Great Hall at Abbots Grange. The picture now hangs at the Tate Gallery in London. Subsequently, the property became a private residence, and more recently, the Grange has become a luxurious award-winning manor house hotel.

---

219. *Mr. E. A. B. Barnard, "Old Days in and Around Evesham."*

The Kettle, an Inn located opposite Tudor House, 65 High Street, renamed the New Inn.[220] It was thought to have run before 1873. Mrs Allard renamed it the **New Inn** when the licence was transferred from the New Inn's original site, the old Midland (subsequently HSBC) Bank, towards the centre of the High Street.

The New Inn was extended in 1891 by Grimmett of Laverton. The landlord was John Cotterill, innkeeper and farmer. He may well have been related to the John Cotterill that lost Tudor House to Stephen Averill in 1852. The landlord in 1914, also called John Cotterill, ran the in as a posting and stabling inn. It is now the **Horse and Hounds.**

Before 1727, The Old Swan Inn, Lower Green. The property was built before 1727. There is a reference to it as the Swan Inn in the Court Leet of that year. It was named after the Swan Meadow, attached to the property, behind the Inn, a large, often waterlogged area in the winter. Swan Meadow was said to have been used by Welsh Drovers en-route from Wales to Smithfield in London. Now walled up, the archway for the passage of carriages, and a reception hall, led to a sizeable, pitched courtyard at the rear. There are a range of previous, now converted, stabling lofts bearing the date 1791 and the studio, dated 1795, is known to have been the site of the coach house. The Inn was converted to a residence in 1791 by John Russell and named after him. The name Swan Inn and licence moved to two cottages across the road, which were extended to create the Swan Hotel, we see today. Historic England identifies Russell House as built around 1791 with later 19th Century additions as little of the former building remains except perhaps the former coach house/barn, to the west, converted into a drawing room and studio. Much of the house over the years has been significantly redesigned. Frank Millet, the American artist who lived there, tragically died when the Titanic sank in 1912.

---

220. Tudor House is now known as Broadway Museum and Art Gallery.

The Swan Meadow was sold by Bill Keil when he owned Russell House and Swan Meadow, in the mid 20th Century, amidst great controversy, to become the estate known as Lifford Gardens.

Around 1791 The Swan Inn, High Street, two cottages were brought together when the licence of the old Swan Inn moved across the road. Both were extended, and a Victorian facade was added to create a building known as the Swan Hotel in the 19th Century and now the Swan Inn today. Joseph Wheatly was proprietor and licence holder in 1820 – 1840, if not before. J Hawkes put up for sale in August 1840 when he moved to take over duties at Turnpike House, High Street. In 1872 J Brick and his family took over the Inn until 1903 when his wife died and retired to Farnham Villa. In 1899 he advertised: *'First-class Family & Commercial J. BRICK Proprietor. Good Accommodation for Visitors at moderate charges. Ales, Wines and Spirits of the Best Quality. Posting of every description.'*[221] The Swan has a fascinating history. Dorothy and William Moon ran in in 1926. As late as 1924, it was the site of one of the three last original signposts in Broadway. The murder of a vulnerable guest was conceived and implemented from the hotel. It has been known for its parties and dances. The Boxing Day Hunt meeting was held at the Swan in the '60s, and in 2018 there was controversy over its outside drinking pods: 'the beach huts!'

19th Century

Before 1805 The Boot was an Inn on the site of the Cotswold Arcade facing the High Street today, part of which included the yard of Cotswold House. This area later became the site of Whittaker's garage. The Boot was kept in 1805 by Stephen Stanley, in 1820 by John Castle, in 1861 by George Newman.

---

221. Bentley's Directory 1899.

The Crown and Trumpet, located on Chapel Street, now named Church Street, is still thriving. The property is thought to have existed since the early 17th Century but was improved in the 19th Century.[222] It appears to have traded as a beerhouse then a public house since 1840, around 180 plus years, possibly a little longer. Between 1871 – 1881 it was known as the Trumpet; this could have been the case on either side of these dates. In 1880, Mrs Mary Hill, the Trumpet's joint innkeeper with her husband Richard, lived there with their four children. She tried to get a licence for a booth at the Willersey Wake. Her application was refused as she did not live in the County (Gloucestershire).[223] Giles Stephenson was an innkeeper in 1881. Edith and John Kennelwell ran it in 1926.

From 1837, The Coach and Horses, High Street. This Inn and Hotel was originally a farm, which became an inn, then a hotel.[224] *COACH & HORSES HOTEL, High Street – W Roberts proprietor. Every accommodation for visitors, cyclists, &c. Waggonettes, traps, on hire. Wines, ales, stout and spirits of the best quality.*
In the mid 20th Century, it was converted into individual cottages. When an inn, it also ran as a livery and carrier business. Local coaches ran passengers to Evesham and Cheltenham. 1851 and 1855, Edward Stephens is recorded as the innkeeper.[225] In 1880 the innkeeper was Charles Allcock, and in 1896, William Roberts. Along with other inns in the village: the Lygon, the Swan, the Angel, the New Inn, it ran regular auctions concerning goods and property. The Harris's ran in in 1926.

Before 1840 The White Horse. Run by Israel Charlwood and later Amelia Turbill. The area where this was located is now part of Orchard Close. When the White Horse was demolished, the site was used to build a private house called 'Ivy Bank'. The house too has been demolished.

---

222. Historic England listing 1214388
223. Gloucestershire Chronicle - Saturday 5 June 1880.
224 . Bennetts Directory 1899
225. 1851 Census.

The Baker's Arms, originally a beerhouse, was part of the Lygon cottages, owned by Martha and William Stanley. After 1861[226] family members defined themselves as agricultural workers; the head of the family was a Farm Bailiff. The property kept its name for a period after transferring its licence to a property in Chapel Street, now Church Street. In 1912 the licence was transferred from Thomas Alfred Harris to George Marshall, though Harris is still the name in 1914, possibly because Marshall has left for the front? One of the last landlords was Giles Stephens. When the property stopped being a beerhouse, it became a private residence called Old Lullington. Finally, the property's name was changed to the Lodge and subsequently to Bannits.

The Butcher's Arms on the High Street was kept by George Stanley, a publican, in 1841[227], then his widow in 1851, but she was described as a beerhouse keeper. It was cottages by the early 20th Century.

The Fox Inn, in Fox Yard, **High Street,** is thought to be either the house or the wine merchants linked to Arnolds of Broadway or Fox House.

The Laurels site is unknown.

Broom Inn, 1899 innkeeper W Harknett

20th Century

1935, Broadway Hotel, on the Green, a complex building with medieval timber-framed elements dating to the 14th Century. It comprises several different properties brought together as one and included Tanyard cottages, or Tan Yard, where hides were turned into leather. One remains part of the Broadway Hotel, and the others are Almshouses. The main building was thought previously to have been a farmhouse on the estate of the Abbots of Pershore. A smithy /blacksmith was part of the building in the late 18th Century. It

---

226. 1861 Census.
227. 1841/1851 Census.

became a bakery in 1831 owned by a Willersey farmer (Caleb Burrows). It was sold as a dwelling house, with bakehouse to a Mrs Holcroft in 1896. Due to it being covered with Ivy, the house was known as Ivy House. The property ceased being a bakery when it changed hands in 1926. The ivy was removed between 1929 and 1932, and the dwelling was renamed The Hollyhocks. It first opened as a hotel in 1935 when two gentlemen purchased it. Subsequent owners have been Mrs Ruddle 1950-1972, Mr Allan 1972-1995, and Cotswold Inns and Hotels Ltd 1995. We must not forget how well Andrew Riley ran in for a short period in the '90s.

Hunters Lodge, originally thought to have been a farmhouse, was a fantastic restaurant with a continental slant run by the Friedli's in the 80's accommodation in the mid 20th Century.

Russell's Restaurant with accommodation, converted 2005 was originally Sands Farmhouse, then later became part of the Gordon Russell office and factory complex. The timber element of the building attached to the main restaurant is said to have come from a building in Worcester.

3. Ale then Beer Houses

Beerhouse, Evesham Road, 1861 Thomas Clark ran a beerhouse and a carrier business. His wife looked after their six children.

The Blackbird, **69 High Street**, was located between the Bindery Gallery and Keytes Lane and possibly accessed from Keytes Lane. Baldwin Morris was the beer seller at the end of the 18th Century.

The Ewe and Lamb, **circa 1820 – 1855,** was kept in 1840 by Fanny Meadows. It was located somewhere near the stables of Mr Jeffery, who owned the house in 1924.

The Gate, a beer seller at the extremity of the village owned by the Leadon Fischer family, is said to have become a cottage at the Leadons before it became Leedons, a mobile home park.

The George, also known as **The Royal Exchange**, was located opposite the Fox & Dog. Arguably, it could have been the property with the double bow window (an Artist studio in the late 20th Century). The overseers of Broadway (parish councillors) are said to have met there in 1725.

The Farmer's Glory, High Street, was run from a residential part of the Midland Stores. In 1840 the beer seller was Mary Stanley.

1855 Fox & Dog, beyond Pond Close, **High Street** Beer sellers traded here in 1840 and 1873. The location may be the group of houses /properties clustered around Halfway House, which was as one property, a stunning B & B in the late 20th Century and is now separate properties; some are owned, others are holiday accommodation. It may well be that the licence, at some point, moved down the road from the Fox Inn

The Malt Shovel 58a High Street was kept by Benjamin Smith in 1840. Later it became a malt house.

The Red Lion was a beerhouse in 1840, which became W G Alexander's surgery by 1924, suggesting the site was **part of Pond Close**.

The Spinning Wheel, China Square, to the left of the entrance to Springfield Lane. Records show a duck stealer was apprehended at the Spinning Wheel in 1774. The beerhouse was converted to cottages by 1924. It is not known if existing cottages link to the original beer house.

The Woolpack stood on the site of Tower View House and was colloquially known as 'Ketch 'em at the end.' There is a suggestion it was older than the Swan. The first licence holder was William Abday, a wool comber, hence the house's name. The licence was dropped before the old house was pulled down in 1911. It was thought to have been located towards Evesham, past the Swan.

4. Cider Houses

Barn House, part of, High Street, next to the Bakery, previously called **Stone Steps**. It was kept in 1880 by Richard Keen.
Cowley House – no more is known.

Hawstead House, formerly Wychwood House, was originally a much smaller 17th Century property called **The Milking Pail,** licenced as a cider house some time up to 1900. It was said to be a favourite establishment of carters from Snowshill. Robert Guthrie held the licence from 1840. The building was extended in the 18th Century then significantly altered in the late 19th Century by Prentice when it became a private house.

Milestones. The licence was held in 1870 by Richard Long, a cider retailer, who bought the licence from The Gables (Grey Gables). Milestones was run as a guest house by Mrs Darley for several years and in the 20th Century, in the '90s as an Italian restaurant.

Rogues' Hall is possibly located in Church/Chapel Street, but the location is unknown. This may have been a colloquial name for the Trumpet?

Tuck Mill, Childswickham Road – had a reputation for drunkenness and disorder, patrons falling asleep in the afternoon under the walnut tree. Occupied by the Crump Family and was said to have sold beer in 1875; however, this is debatable, as it was refused a licence to become an alehouse in 1895.

5. Maltsters

Smith, Benjamin – no more is known. Ann Smith was a Maltster in 1820

White Stephen, maltster at the Lygon Arms 1841. The White's seemed to have been Maltsters, father to son, independently for many years 1716 – 1822.

Known Carriers/Livery. [228]

1820 White, William Junior.
1861 Clark, Thomas Evesham Road.
Hawkes, Joseph born 1796, licenced to let gigs and horses – insolvent 1841 his wife's name was Bright.
1899 Crump, High Street.
      Drury S North Cotswold Mews, The Sands
      Knight E, High Street.
      Price C, Pentheul Lodge High Street, Horses, and carriages for hire; also, apartments.
1914 Jacques WG.
      Knight, E.

---

[228] Worcestershire General and Commercial Directory, 1820. Bentley's Directory 1899,

Appendix 2

An Index to the Statutes at Large: From Magna Carta to the Forty-Ninth Year of George III Inclusive, Volume 1 by John Raithby, Esq. of Lincoln's Inn, Barrister at Law. Printed by George Erre and Andrew Srathan, Printers to the King's Most Law, Printer to the King's Most Excellent Majesty. 1814

Alehouses.
Common Inns, Proviso for,
Common selling of Ale and Beer in Alehouses, Justices may remove,
Constable neglecting to punish.
Continuance of Licence, recorded,
Continuing drinking in Alehouses
Conviction certified to Quarter Sessions;
Copies of Recognizances delivered. See Clerk of the Peace.
Disabled from selling Ale, disabled also from felling Spirituous Liquors,
Double Punishments, not to be.
Dying or Removing, Licence to Successor,
Ecclesiastical Jurisdiction, Proviso.
Entering upon Profession of licenced Houses, without Authority of Justices, 32 Evidence of Parishioners
Executors of Alehouse Keepers dying, new Licence.
Fairs, having for
Forfeitures, how disposed of,
Former Laws, in force,
General Issue,
Justices, adjourning Trial,
Jurisdiction of, in common Alehouses,
Suspecting unlicenced Persons, Proceedings,
Keeping Alehouses. See Licence. Unlicenced.
Licence, Alehouse, keeping, without,
Alehouse Keeper not having, selling Beer,
Fees to Commissioners, for, none,
Notice of granting, 26 Stamps for Duties, Regulations,
Successor may keep Licence,
Licenced Alehouses, deemed Places for reading. See Seditious Societies, tit.
Alehouses.
London, times of granting Licences in Middlesex, licencing, Meetings for
Oath of Constable, to present Offences, Offences Where determined, Petty Sessions, new Licences, granting; at
Prisons,4 Alehouses.
Aliens. *Prisons,* selling Ale, &c. in, licenced,
Prosecutions, Limitation of,
Recognizances of Alehouse Keepers,
Clerk of the Peace, sent to,

Beer and Ale

deemed concealed Places, *ib.*
Retailers, travelling to make Entries,
Strong Beer, / what deemed,
"Table Beer, S c.81. 5 12.
Table Beer, Storehouses for, Entry of, in what cafe,
Witnesses, not attending Justices,
Excise Office, Entries to be made at, 12 Car. 2. c. 24. | 29. Times of Entry regulated,} 630.
Exportation, Bounty (Strong Beer, &c.), 1 G.3. *C.7.* 96.
Clapboard to be imported for Beer exported, 35 El.c. 11. 52.
Colonies, to, Proviso for,
Drawback, Oath by Brewer, for obtaining,
Penalty for exporting,
Licence, to exhibit, to Officer, 5G.3. C. 46.
Copy, to suffer to be made, 20. Places used for laying in Beer, Entry of, 35 G.3. c. 113.
Spirits, drinking out of Retailer's House
 Vessels marked according to Standard, to sell in, how made,
1*Ships going to foreign Parts,* Beer, &c, for Use of, Proviso for,
Small Beer. See *Table Beer.*
Strong Beer. See *Excise.*
Table Beer, Excise, Allowances,
Casks, marked,
Mixing with Strong Beer or Worts,
Separate from other Beer, kept,
Vessels containing more than three Barrels, Brewer putting Table Beer into, $11.
Universities, Proviso for, respecting Measures of Beer and Ale,
Vessels marked by Standard Measure, Beer, &c. to be sold in,
Mayors, &c. to provide, *Warrants*
Beer and Ale.
Warrants by Justices for seizing. See *Excise,* tit. Licences. Wormwood in {Beer,} Ann. c. 12.
Beggars with Children. See Rogues and Vagabonds.

Bibliography
Print.

Alfred the Great, *The Anglo-Saxon Chronicles,* Pantianos Classics, 2008 - paperback edition

Allan Fea, *Nooks and Corners of Old England*, Secker, 1910.

Allen, Loise. *Stage coach Travel*, Shire Publications, Illustrated edition, 10 July 2014

Barnard Mr. E. A. B, *"Old Days in and Around Evesham."*

Calder, A. *Three Cotswold Architects,* Alan Calder Press, 2020

Cornish, Tony and Plant James Plant, *Aberystwyth - a photographic history of your town*, Black Horse Books, 2001.

Fiennes, Celia *Through England on a side saddle in the Times of William and Mary,* London: Field and Tuer, The Leadenhall Press, 1888.

Goodman Kevin, *Disease, and Illness in the Black Country, Volume I, Medieval to Early Medieval*, Bows, Blades and Battles Press, 2020

Gordon, Catherine. *The Coventry's of Croome,* Phillimore & Co Ltd, First Edition, 31 Dec. 2000

Gordon, Catherine. *Cotswold Arts and Architecture,* The History Press, 2nd edition 2020

Habington, Thomas. Ed. Amphlett, John. *A Survey of Worcestershire;* (Edited for the Worcestershire Historical Society,) Volumes 1 & 2, The Oxford Press, 1896.

Harper, Charles G. *The Holyhead Road Vol 1, The Mail-Coach Road to Dublin*, Chapman, and Hall Limited, 1902.

Harper, Charles G. *Stage coach and Mail in Days of Yore, a picturesque history of the coaching age Volume 1.* Chapman and Hall, Limited, 1903.

Hindle, Paul. *Medieval Roads and Tracks,* Shire Publications, second revised edition, 2008

Houghton, Colin, *Broadway Pictorial*, Darien-Jones Publishing, 1987

Unknown Author, Hudson of Wick, Page 212

Hughes, Charles. *Shakespeare's Europe; unpublished chapters of Fynes Moryson's Itinerary, being a survey of the condition of Europe at the end of the 16th Century,* 1903 (Sherratt and Hughes. London) Ingram, Rev James, Giles, Dr.J.A. (Translators)

James, John Hissey, *Travels in a Dog Cart*, Richard Bentley, 1st Edition, 1891

James, John Hissey, *Travels around England in a Dog Cart, and Leisurely Tour in England,* MacMillan, and Co, Ltd 1913

Hyde, J Wilson: *The Post in Grant and Farm*, Adam and Charles Black, London 1894

King, Carole, The Rise and Decline of Village Reading Rooms, Rural History, 20(2) page 163, 2009

Knight Charles, *The Penny Magazine*, Charles Knight publisher, editor, and author 1832 issue

Laird, *A Topographical and Historical Description of the County of Worcester*, Sherwood, Neely, and Jones, Paternoster Row; and George Cowie and Co. 1814.

Moore, Jerold Northrop, *F.L. Griggs, The Architecture of Dreams,* Clarendon Press, Oxford, 1999

Lipson. E. *The History of Wool and its Manufacture,* (Mainly in England) (William Heineman Ltd) 1953

Mountfield, David. *Stage and Mail Coaches,* Shire Library (Shire Library. Bloomsbury Ltd.) 2009

Payne, W.H. *The costume of Great Britain* 1804, printed for William Miller, by William Bulmer & Co.

Palmer, John, in J. Wilson Hyde, *One Hundred Years by Post*, Sampson Low, Marston & Co,

Pepys, *The Diaries of Samuel Pepys: A selection*, Penguin Books

Pevsner, Nikolaus, *The Buildings of England,* Penguin Books, 1951

Power, Eileen. *The Wool Trade in English Medieval History* being the Ford Lectures Eileen Power Professor of Economic History in the University of London. (Oxford University Press 1941)

Raithby, John Esq. Lincoln's Inn, Barrister at Law, *An Index to the Statutes at Large: From Magna Carta to the Forty-Ninth Year of George III Inclusive, Volume 1* George Erre and Andrew Srathan, Printers to the King's Most Law, Printer to the King's Most Excellent Majesty. 1814

Saville, Chris (2019) Student dissertation for the Open University module A329. *The Making of Welsh history. Did John Ogilby complicitly map a route from Aberystwyth to London as part of clandestine plans for a Catholic invasion of England and Wales, at the behest of Charles II?* Page 7.

Stow, John. : *A Summarie of the Chronicles of England Diligently Collected, Abridged, & Continued Unto this Present Yere of Christ* 1598.

Stow, William. (Eds. Norris, T & Tracy, H) *Remarks on London: 1722. Being an Exact Survey of the Cities of London and Westminster, Borough of Southwark, and the Suburbs and Liberties Contiguous to Them, ...* (Norris and Tracy with permission from the original copy held at Oxford University) 1722

Souden David: *The Journals of the Hon. John Byng*, 1781–1792, edited 1991.

Symonds Richard, *Diaries of the Marches of the Royal Army, 10 April 1644 – 11 February 1645,* First published from the original manuscripts in the British Museum, Nichols and sons, printers, 1859

Tomalin, Claire. *Diary of Samuel Pepys and Samuel Pepys, The unequalled Self, (Penguin 2012)*

Toulson, Shirley *The Drovers*, Shire Books, 2005.

Viner, David. *Wagons and Carts,* Shire Library Publications, Bloomsbury Ltd. 2008.

Wright, Geoffrey, N. *Turnpike Roads,* Shire Library, 2000

Media. and Archives online.
BBC History:
https:www/bbc.c.uk/history/British/middle/ages/black/death

The British Postal Museum & Archive *The Mail Coach Service, https://www.google.com/search*

http://www.bonsonhistory.co.uk/html/hoxton___shoreditch

Gascoigne, Bamber *HistoryWorld History of Transport and Travel*.

Glyn Redworth, Ben Coates, *The History of Parliament Volumes: https://www.historyofparliamentonline.org/volume/ 1604-1629/constituencies/droitwich*

Harleian Manuscripts in the British Museum
https://www.bl.uk/collection- guides/harley-manuscripts

History of the Cotswold Hunt. www.cotswoldhunt.co.uk.

https://Historyhouse.co.uk/articles/window_tax.html

https://www.igg.org.uk/gansg/12-linind/milk.html

Nassif, Kristen. *An Artists' Colony in Broadway, Worcestershire: 1885-1889. WordPress.com.*

Oxford Journal/Cheltenham Examiner/ Evesham Journal/Evesham and Standard and West Midlands Observer/Worcestershire Chronicle/ Worcester News/ Gloucestershire Chronicle *https://www.britishnewspaperarchive.co.uk*

Thurloe, John. Ed. Birch T. A *Collection of the State Papers of John Thurloe, Volume 1, 1638-1653*, https://www.british-history.ac.uk/thurloe- papers/vol1

Maps
1776 - Andrews J, & Drury A, *a new travelling map of the Country round London, the route Broadway, Evesham, Worcester, Bromyard, and Wales.*
Aspin J Lavoisne's Atlas, Principal High Roads
Ogilby, J *1675 Strip Road Map- section across the Vale of Evesham Worcestershire maps: 1883, 1900, 1921,*